D0709579

Connecting with South Africa

Number Sixteen

CAROLYN AND ERNEST FAY SERIES
IN ANALYTICAL PSYCHOLOGY

David H. Rosen, General Editor

The Carolyn and Ernest Fay edited book series, based initially on the annual Fay Lecture Series in Analytical Psychology, was established to further the ideas of C. G. Jung among students, faculty, therapists, and other citizens and to enhance scholarly activities related to analytical psychology. The Book Series and Lecture Series address topics of importance to the individual and to society. Both series were generously endowed by Carolyn Grant Fay, the founding president of the C. G. Jung Educational Center in Houston, Texas. The series are in part a memorial to her late husband, Ernest Bel Fay. Carolyn Fay has planted a Jungian tree carrying both her name and that of her late husband, which will bear fruitful ideas and stimulate creative works from this time forward. Texas A&M University and all those who come in contact with the growing Fay Jungian tree are extremely grateful to Carolyn Grant Fay for what she has done. The holder of the McMillan Professorship in Analytical Psychology at Texas A&M functions as the general editor of the Fay Book Series.

A list of titles in this series appears at the end of the book.

Connecting with South Africa

Cultural Communication and Understanding

ASTRID BERG

Texas A&M University Press   College Station

Copyright © 2012 by Astrid Berg
Manufactured in the United States of America
All rights reserved
First edition

This paper meets the requirements of ANSI/NISO Z39.48–1992
(Permanence of Paper).
Binding materials have been chosen for durability.

LIBRARY OF CONGRESS CATALOGING-IN-PUBLICATION DATA

Berg, Astrid, 1950–
Connecting with South Africa : cultural communication and understanding /
Astrid Berg. — 1st ed.
p. cm. — (Carolyn and Ernest Fay series in analytical psychology ; no. 16)
Includes bibliographical references and index.
ISBN-13: 978-1-60344-430-9 (cloth : alk. paper)
ISBN-10: 1-60344-430-0 (cloth : alk. paper)
ISBN-13: 978-1-60344-580-1 (e-book)
ISBN-10: 1-60344-580-3 (e-book)
1. Social psychology—South Africa.   2. Psychoanalysis and culture—
South Africa.   3. Psychoanalysis and racism—South Africa.   4. Infant
psychology—South Africa.   5. Developmental psychology—South Africa.
6. Jungian psychology—South Africa.   7. South Africa—Social life and
customs—21st century.   8. Ubuntu (Philosophy)   9. Group identity—South
Africa.   10. Intercultural communication—South Africa. I. Title. II. Series:
Carolyn and Ernest Fay series in analytical psychology ; no. 16.
HM1027.S6B47   2012
302.0968—dc23
2011016694

Cover and frontispiece art by Thobile Skepe; used by permission.

Contents

Series Editor's Foreword

> With African *Ubuntu* philosophy, the entire planet is
> viewed as a living being.
>
> —C. G. Jung

Astrid Berg's progressive book, *Connecting with South Africa: Cultural Communication and Understanding,* based on her presentation at the twentieth anniversary of the Carolyn and Ernest Fay Lecture Series in Analytical Psychology, is an integration of personal (subjective) and collective (objective) material. Through Astrid's honest account we learn about her healing journey and South Africa's transformation from apartheid to democracy, led by Nelson Mandela. She stayed in South Africa and was there during its truth and reconciliation period, which is significant given that whites comprise only 10 percent of the population. Astrid's openness and courage enabled her to confront and overcome her inner racism and fear. She has owned her own shame and guilt as well as become a devoted helper and healer of the less fortunate and downtrodden in her beloved motherland. In a real way, Astrid reminds me of Eleanor Roosevelt, who also gave so much of herself to our country and the world community. Astrid was inspired by her mentor, Vera Bührmann (1984), also a child psychiatrist and the first Jungian analyst in South Africa. Astrid focuses on the most vulnerable of the inhabitants of South Africa: the children. She became an expert in infant mental health and in 1995 hosted the first world conference on this vital topic in South Africa. Astrid gives infants the status of whole human beings, which parallels how she views her fellow citizens in South Africa through conscious caring and the philosophy of *ubuntu*. Her text is a beacon of hope for infants and the new South Africa, building bridges and blending the art of healing with the science of understanding. Astrid brings feeling and compassion to psychology and psychiatry, fields that have been dominated for so long by reason and thinking. This volume is a scientific foundation of analytical psychology as well as a bold, spirited memoir.

Why connect with South Africa? Using the hologram model, this nation represents all of Africa, and we need to dialogue and interact with our brothers and sisters in the continent where we originated. C. G. Jung challenged us to address the two-million-year-old-self within (1965). How are we to do this? Jung, who visited Africa, suggested that we embrace our dreams where the ancestors are ever present. As Astrid shows, dreams and healing rituals are linked to the ancestors and the collective unconscious. Jung maintained that we are suffering from loss of soul (1955), on both the individual and world levels. Astrid's work is about reconnecting with soul, bridge building, and realizing that we are all interconnected in a global village.

It is noteworthy that Sir Laurens van der Post left South Africa and, from exile in London, spoke out against apartheid. He knew Jung and wrote one of the best books about him (1976). Frank McMillan Jr., who brought Jung's psychology to Texas (in the southern part of the United States), knew and corresponded with Sir Laurens van der Post. After Sir Laurens's death, the McMillan family established a library named after Frank McMillan at the Jung Centre in Cape Town. It has become the premier resource for psychoanalytic literature in all of Africa.

In her moving introduction, Astrid sees South Africa as a microcosm of the rest of the world and asks us to consider the other as equal. However, she outlines many problems in South Africa, such as poverty and crime caused by modernization and rapid changes in the society. And she is wary about the wholesale adoption of western standards and the loss of old cultural values. Astrid also records the growth and development of analytical (Jungian) psychology in South Africa. In chapter 1, "Building Bridges: Infants and Parents in a Cape Town Community," she outlines the arduous beginning of an infant clinic in Khayelitsha, a South African township. Chapter 2, "And What about the Infant?" is a biopsychosocial treatise concerning the infant in breadth and depth, and it includes a clinical case. Chapter 3, "The Baby's Name Was Not Understood: A Case of Failed and Successful Mother-Infant Psychotherapy," teaches us about a difficult but healing case in which a huge mistake—which fortunately turns out well—allows us to learn. This material underscores how essential it is to understand cultural attitudes and the value of healing relationships. The fourth chapter, "Ancestor Reverence," lays the groundwork for discerning healing rituals and comprehending *ubuntu*. In chapter 5, "An Adolescent Rite of Passage: What Can We Learn from African Culture?" we are immersed in the fascinating initiation of boys into manhood. Chapter 6, "*Ubuntu*: An African Contribution to the 'Civilization as a Whole,'" is the basis of forgiveness and the truth and reconciliation process, which has come to characterize South Africa. The book ends with a touching afterword.

In sum, I have nothing but praise for this one-of-a-kind volume and its hopeful philosophy of *ubuntu*, which can only promote meaningful connection with South Africa, leading to peace and the conscious evolution of our human family on Mother Earth.

David H. Rosen
College Station, Texas

References

Bührmann, V. 1984. *Living in Two Worlds.* Cape Town, South Africa: Human and Rousseau.

Jung, C. G. 1965. *Memories, Dreams, and Reflections.* New York: Vintage Books.

———. 1955. *Modern Man in Search for a Soul.* New York: Harcourt Harvest.

van der Post, Sir Laurens. 1976. *Jung and the Story of Our Time.* New York: Vintage Books.

Acknowledgments

Carolyn Fay needs to be thanked first of all for her vision in establishing the Fay Lectures. It was a particular honor for me to have been the twentieth lecturer in this series. That it is hosted by Texas A&M University gives it particular importance: that a university excelling in medicine, in the sciences, in mechanics and engineering should have a space for the humanities and in particular for in-depth psychological studies is to be admired, and it gives this series a special significance. I thank Carolyn Fay and I thank the university for having enabled these lectures to take place.

A very warm thank-you from me to David Rosen, McMillan Professor of Analytical Psychology at this university; without his doing, his initiative, none of the ideas or wishes of Carolyn Fay would have been realized. I thank him for his warm hospitality and careful looking after on many levels.

Then I would like to thank the people of South Africa, to whom this book is dedicated. Without their generosity of spirit, their sincerity and openness, I would not be who I am today. Particular thanks go to Nosisana Nama, my colleague, mentor, and friend, whose loyalty and support is unwavering; also to Elizabeth Qoba, who fulfills the additional mothering functions in my home—my many informal conversations with her have helped me form a more nuanced, composite picture of her inner world and possibly of that of many, many others. Vera Bührmann, who had mentored me over many years, prepared me for this work—whether she was aware of this or not, I will never know; I thank her and honor her as one of my ancestors. I will refer to her and her work throughout the book.

I would like to thank my colleagues in the Division of Child and Adolescent Psychiatry at the University of Cape Town, and in particular my colleague, Professor Alan Flisher, whose untimely death shortly after my return from giving the lectures has left us bereft. His and my colleagues' trust in me, leaving me to do what I felt strongly about, has given me the space to develop my interest. Alan's continued prodding to write it all up was a great motivating factor for me.

Last and most deeply I want to thank my family: my husband Heinz Rode and my two adult children, Maja and Hagen, who have always been encouraging and supportive, who never complained when I was preoccupied, and who always understood my passion. Without them I would not have been able to do this.

Connecting with South Africa

Introduction

What constitutes man's greatness is his being a
bridge and not an end.
                    —F. Nietzsche, *Also sprach Zarathustra*

The unique qualities and defining realities of South Africa derive from
its rich plurality of languages and cultures. Of its nearly 50 million inhabitants more than three quarters are black Africans, 10 percent are
white, and 10 percent are Indian and so-called Coloured (of mixed
race). There are eleven official languages. Its history is turbulent—a colonial past marked by many skirmishes and wars, followed by nearly fif-
ty years of Apartheid rule and then the dismantling of that regime and
the coming together of a nation. The post-Mandela era has not been so
easy, politically speaking, and many challenges face the country.

What is refreshing and hopeful is the fact that the debates in the
country are vigorous and robust—South Africa has a free press and
no shortage of material for talented cartoonists and satirists. It is a
fact that there is now majority rule, but it is also true that the white
minority continues to have the economic wealth and clout and the lifestyle aspired to by many, particularly young people. Slowly a powerful
black middle class is emerging, and in them is where the stability of the
country lies. The gains of this, however, may also mean a loss—a loss
of a meaningful old culture, part of which is a theme in this book.

Because of its troubled past and peaceful transition, because of the friendliness of its peoples, its natural beauty, and its diversity, South Africa can get under one's skin, so to speak. Once people have visited they tend to come back, time and again. But, one may ask, what might be the relevance of South Africa to the rest of the world? Why should a Fay Lecture Series revolve around a country at the tip of the African continent? And more specifically, why should young children, indeed infants, be of interest and why should an intercultural focus be of significance to an audience and readership so far away?

South Africa is a microcosm—what has happened and what is happening there occurs in many places in the world, and in many of those places there is not peace but war and bloodshed. What we as white South Africans are asked to do is what is required of the western world: to step down from the place of superiority and become equal with the "other." It is incumbent on us as the past privileged group to acknowledge and reach out; to see what we were not allowed to see, and to feel what we had defended against. The western world is undeniably more advanced in certain areas of science and economic development, but in other areas it seems to lag behind and could learn from other groups in the rest of the world.

The style of this lecture series is one that invites moving with me from inner subjective experience to outer objective reality, from feelings engendered within to scientific reasoning and scholarly thinking without.

The core narrative is about making connections, about building bridges between self and other. In order to do this, the self—that is, my subjectivity—has a place alongside the objectivity of the other. The other includes of course the people with whom I work, be they patients or colleagues, but it also includes the objectivity of scientific findings in the field of early human development and the scholarly contributions made in the area of African culture.

What follows is thus a subjective account, situating myself in the South African context, which represents a personal but also a collective position; at the same time the work is a scientific discourse regarding infant development and is also scholarly in terms of intercultural thinking.

The task is to hold the tension between this subjective and objective, between involvement and detachment. In that sense it is truly psychoanalytic as it is this kind of interplay on which analytic theory and practice is built.

I hope these lectures will be a contribution toward the realization that in the smallest, the most vulnerable, there lies the hope for the future; that bridges to the other can be built, even in the face of historical divides and inequalities; that western culture is not superior to other cultures and that we can all learn from one another, thereby celebrating the world's diversity.

Bridge Builders in South Africa

To build a bridge means to create a structure that spans and provides a passage over a gap or barrier—it is about connecting self with the other, and this is a profoundly human task.

In this particular work it was contact with infants that proved enabling for me in reaching out to the other in a country that has experienced injustice, inhumanity, and violent repression and has managed to move beyond without further bloodshed.

South Africa contains many individuals who have been bridge builders—the most famous examples being Nelson Mandela and Archbishop Desmond Tutu. But there are many, many others: from academics and corporate people to the man in the street and the woman in her home. It is to them, the ordinary people, that I pay my respects, because they get no accolades for being those bridges—they do it because they are human beings, and they are the ones who make up the story that is to follow.

I also want to pay tribute to Dr. Vera Bührmann, who was a bridge builder far ahead of her time. I came to know her during my psychiatric registrar days in 1976, just as she was retiring from her clinical practice at the Red Cross War Memorial Children's Hospital in Cape Town, where she had worked as a child psychiatrist. She had been greatly concerned about the difficulties autistic children and their families were facing, and she was instrumental in establishing the first special school for autistic children in Cape Town—today called the Vera School, in her honor.

In her retirement she took another road—not that of autistic non-communication and aloneness but its opposite: exploring the belief system of her fellow South African citizens who were black; working to understand the religious and cultural encounters people have with each other and with their universe. It was quite a jump away from the autistic shell of the troubled children she saw.

Vera Bührmann was a bridge builder far ahead of her time, showing the way by crossing multiple boundaries and opening herself up to the other. She is pictured with her interpreter Joseph Gqomfa in 1991, after she received an honorary doctorate from the University of Cape Town.

The South Africa of the 1970s and –80s was a very different place from the one known today—when Vera traveled into the rural area of the officially designated "homeland" of a group of amaXhosa people, she was crossing more than one boundary. Geographically she went into a region that was forbidden territory for whites (she required a special permit every time she went); she lived with and communicated intimately with a black African community; and she crossed language barriers—although she had grown up on a farm and had known isiXhosa since her childhood, she also always had an interpreter with her. And beyond these boundaries, she crossed over to and opened herself up to the other—through her participant observation she became a bridge builder.

She lived in an old Volkswagen bus during this time—a kombi-camper she bought from one of our colleagues was her home into which she retreated to gather herself. One cannot research African traditions in a nonparticipant, "outside" kind of way—one has to enter into the process oneself. The ancestors are always asked whether it is in order for this visitor to be there, and then it is incumbent on the visitor to participate, to partake in the ritual beer drinking, clapping, and singing. These occasions can go on for many hours, right through the night, and I can well imagine the exhaustion she must have felt on returning to her VW bus.

Vera participated fully, but she also recorded, and then transcribed and had translated what she had heard and experienced. This was qualitative research at its best. Throughout her writing she shows her clarity of thought and her honesty. She never made grand, sweeping statements; she would always be quite specific in saying she was talking about a particular group of people she had come to know, and that she was describing their way of doing things. The work was never meant to be a portrayal of all black African people.

Yet it is remarkable how accurate and how widely applicable her descriptions are. I have built on them—the basis of my knowledge comes from hearing Vera speak and reading her work, notably her little book *Living in Two Worlds* (Bührmann 1984).

I have continued speaking to others—my patients, work colleagues, and friends. And indeed, what Vera describes holds true today. I have not traveled into rural areas in order to experience traditional ceremonies but have had the good fortune of being able to do so in Cape Town. Through friends I have been invited to join several ceremonies—an *intlombe,* funerals, an *imbeleko,* and a *goduka* ceremony, some of which are described later. And although these were conducted in the city, all the essential elements that Vera described are there; if they are not there, you can know that something is very wrong.

Vera did not create these ceremonies; she brought them into non-African consciousness. Because she was thorough and careful, and because she had authentic and deep respect for the people whom she observed, she got at the truth of these ceremonies. This kind of truth does not simply go away, nor is it easily swayed by modern, urban, global western culture. It remains deeply embedded. Whenever I get worried that something of this precious worldview may get lost, I am reassured by my friends that the ancestors are stronger than this and that they will stay.

My theoretical introduction to transcultural work came from Vera, but the impetus to discover more for myself came from a different quarter—it came from the baby, from my profession as a child psychiatrist. It was the infants themselves who formed the bridge to the mothers, to the clinic staff, and to the community; it was through the infant that I became aware of a rich culture—one I did not have the privilege of getting to know during my childhood or early adulthood.

The link to the infant is a constant in this book, though I move beyond the infants themselves. The archetypal pattern or thread around which all of this is woven is the to and fro alternation of "from small to big and from big to small." It is imperative that we keep both in mind: that in the smallest movement during early life lies the kernel of potential greatness, and in all greatness there is a small, simple beginning that should never be forgotten.

I would like to start on a personal note by briefly situating myself in the context being described. This story is one of many examples of people finding their way to make a contribution to a country that is riveting in its complexity and humanity.

The Personal Equation

Lee Roloff was a good friend of Vera Bührmann and a good friend of the Southern African Association of Jungian Analysts. In fact, he was a key figure in the organization's birth. He visited frequently and has maintained his contact with us, even going to the considerable effort to come to Cape Town for the 2007 conference of the International Association for Analytical Psychology.

Roloff had many wise words and we remember them—I particularly remember his assertion: every thesis is a "me-this." While my work is not a thesis in the literal, academic sense, and was not setting out to become that, it has become a life-thesis in the broader sense and in the end is thus also about me.

My mother was a refugee from eastern Prussia and led the last horse-drawn wagon over the bridge of the Weichsel River before it was blown up by bombs. She came to South Africa soon afterward as she could not tolerate being a refugee in western Germany. She met my father, who had come to South Africa from northern Germany before the war; they married and established a family.

Unlike present day black African refugees flocking to South Africa, my parents were not discriminated against—they belonged to the favored group of the then Apartheid government: white Germans! What more could they want? For me as a child this was fortunate: I was able to attend good schools and go to university, something I may well not have had the chance of doing had my mother remained as a farm laborer in postwar Germany. So I benefited from the system, and I have to acknowledge that. I have a deep sense of "owing" the country of my birth.

My conscious realization of Apartheid came gradually at high school but more dramatically at university. I participated in liberal, leftwing student activities and was noted by the Security Police, though never detained. In the 1980s protests were at their height, but I was busy raising two young children while keeping my career going, and I was not politically active during this phase. This is partly a reality, but also an excuse. Militancy was necessary during that time, and head-on confrontation with the security forces was often the only way, but it is something I was not able to do. Through my work I know I was trusted, and I had some professional consultations with members of families involved with the then outlawed and underground African National Congress (ANC, later to become the governing party), but other than that I did not step out of my zone of safety.

However, the tension was unbearable, and my family and I could not have been happier when it all changed: Nelson Mandela walked out of prison in February 1990, giving the forbidden ANC salute—the defining, pivotal moment—which happened as we were celebrating my daughter's tenth birthday. The salute was the beginning of a long path to freedom for all—a path we are still trying to find. This book is testimony to one way of connecting the historical divide.

CHAPTER 1

Building Bridges

INFANTS AND PARENTS IN A
CAPE TOWN COMMUNITY

In April 1994 we had our first democratic elections in South Africa, a triumphant event—active participation by all, and no violence. We were all heady with pride and enthusiasm. In January 1995 I was instrumental in organizing the first Infant Mental Health Conference in South Africa. The idea came from the Jungian child analyst Mara Sidoli: she planted the seed, and she helped me find colleagues to present papers. It was a huge success, and I realized only in retrospect that part of the reason for this success was the synchronicity of talking about real infants in the new, "infant" South Africa.

Beginning at the Beginning

This conference was the start of many creative endeavors in the country: it led to the establishment of associations in infant mental health in Cape Town and Johannesburg, both of which are affiliated with the World Association of Infant Mental Health; it led to a second Conference on Infant Mental Health in 2000, and it led to us being chosen as the hosts for the thirteenth conference of the world association in Cape Town in 2012. A large collaborative research project was set up during this period—looking at the prevalence of postpartum depression and the effect of this depression on the development of the infant—and other projects followed.

What is of relevance here (and close to my heart) is the clinical work with parents and infants to which all this gave rise. I was given the go-ahead by the University of Cape Town in Rondebosch and the head of the Department of Psychiatry to establish a parent-infant mental health service. I was advised by my professor of that time not to limit myself to working from my hospital, the academic base (tertiary health care), but to enter the community and start a service there, at a primary level. I objected to this—I considered myself ill-equipped to work in an unknown, for me "foreign" setting, when I was not at all sure what I was going to do with parents and their infants in a known setting. However, I took to heart his argument that we could not afford, in 1995, in the new South Africa, to be starting a new service that would have been seen to be providing help only to the well-to-do part of the city.

Thus, having accepted that I would have to do both—that is, start the service in a tertiary as well as a primary health care setting—I had to answer the question: what was I, as the person driving this alone, actually going to do? What would I offer and to whom? Infant mental health interventions have different levels and in order to be comprehensive, attention needs to be given to all of them. Prevention and treatment are intimately linked, and the younger the child, the more this holds true. If this intervention is to be done properly and according to the textbook, it requires quantitative research that can influence policy decisions; it then requires clinical trials that measure whether a particular intervention is working from the objective, scientific point of view. It requires different teams working in different settings and ascertaining whether a particular model is effective. And all of this means having almost unlimited resources, both financial and human—neither of which are at my disposal. The challenge for me has been: what can I do, given my constraints in terms of money and professional support?

I decided, or rather I was led to decide by forces outside of my conscious awareness, to be who I am, no matter where I work: that I am both a child psychiatrist and an analyst, and that I regard my basic role as that of a psychotherapist. As a child psychiatrist I center my attention on the infant—it is from him or her that I gather information. As a psychotherapist I do not merely want to gather information, but I want to provide alleviation of suffering—I need to do something with what I observe; and again, the younger the child, the less this is so via conventional medical psychiatry, where a diagnosis is made and medication prescribed. It requires a psychological intervention, an emotional intervention, and thus infant-parent psychotherapy is what I do.

But I am getting ahead of myself. Before one can do anything one has to have a base, a place from which to work. In my hospital clinic setting this was not a problem: I used my office in which to see parents and infants, and I made use of the infrastructure provided by the out-patient department. In the community I had no such base, and obtaining one was an adventure—at times a frightening one.

Entering the Unknown

The work in Rondebosch is much like I imagine work at any child psychiatry unit in Europe. There is a reception area with staff, consulting rooms, playrooms, and a steady team that fills the building. The patients are seen as per appointment, and the week is scheduled to the hour for every person working there. Regular team discussions are held where case material is presented in detail and where academic input is part of the course. The work is reliable, predictable, and known. It is embedded in the long history of similar units all over the western world. I knew that being in a primary health care clinic would offer me none of this, but what I did not know was that I would have to engage in a process, the complexity of which I had not envisioned.

When my professor suggested that I also work in the community I decided to go to a township called Khayelitsha. Black South African townships owe their origins to the Group Areas Act passed in 1950, assigning races to different residential and business sections in urban areas (its effects are summarized at http://www.africanaencyclopedia. com/apartheid/apartheid.html). Slowly but determinedly, all black people were moved out of "white areas"; those who were legally in the urban areas because of having the necessary work permits were then moved into townships adjoining the big cities. Khayelitsha, which means "new home," became an official township in the 1980s and is the third largest of such townships in South Africa. It lies eleven kilometers away from metropolitan Cape Town, adjacent to the international airport. Geographically it is situated in the Cape Flats— lowlands between the mountains of the Cape Peninsula and those of the lush interior wine lands. The Cape Flats offer spectacular views onto both sets of mountain ranges, but on the ground the soil is poor and sandy, growing water-logged because of winter rains or desertlike and dusty because of summer winds.

The inhabitants are Xhosa-speaking people who have moved to the city from their former "homeland," now the Eastern Cape, in search of employment, better education, and health care. Most members of the family, especially the elders, remain behind in the traditional homestead while the young people, young mothers, flock to the urban areas. Housing is in makeshift shelters, which may be turned into houses made of bricks as time passes; currently there are different stages of housing development evident as one drives through. But when one descends by plane from above to land, or when one drives by on the highway, all one sees are shacks: thousands of them, close to each other. They all seem the same, and one does not really want to look and is grateful for the concrete wall erected to prevent people from crossing the road. It is easier to ignore the obvious poverty and drive by swiftly. At this point something needs to be said about the color line that was so deftly drawn by the Apartheid government and that permeates the society to this day.

The Color Line

In the Apartheid days white people were not allowed into black townships such as Khayelitsha. The reasons for these laws were complex but were motivated psychologically by a drive for power, based in part on an unconscious sense of inferiority of the self that manifested in the fear of the other. The other, as a recipient of projections, became condensed into one undifferentiated mass of blackness. A dark skin color became the signifier for a host of psychic attributes: mental inferiority and primitiveness in the widest possible senses of these words. Thus external laws had to be made to keep these perceived threats to "white civilization" at bay. The brutality and thoroughness of the laws of the Apartheid government were such that this split was successfully perpetuated externally as well as internally.

Steelworkers sharing a joke; photograph by Nick Hedges. The core narrative of this book is about making connections, about building bridges between self and the other. "But what if I should discover that the least among them all, the poorest of all beggars, the most impudent of all offenders, yea the very fiend himself—that these are within me . . . that I myself am the enemy who must be loved—what then?" (Jung).

Only when I entered Khayelitsha in 1995 did I became fully aware of how much I had incorporated this racist split. Apartheid had been an effective system indeed. The withdrawal of projections has been an ongoing process for me, and with it strong emotions have come to the surface: emotions of fear, shame, and guilt. I have had to acknowledge these within myself and I am sure that this process is one that people in South Africa have had to go through and are still going through. Fear of otherness was manifested concretely in my complete unfamiliarity with the physical layout of Khayelitsha. Going into such an unknown area meant facing physical uncertainty on many levels, including about being violated in one way or another. It also involved having to face the poverty I had only read about in newspapers and had preferred to ignore. When, after a while, I came to know the area and some of the people living there, my fear soon gave way to shame that, as an educated person, I had been completely ignorant of my fellow citizens' lifestyle, customs, and values.

Finding a Space

During all my time in Khayelitsha—from 1995 to the present—I have been accompanied and led by two special women: Nosisana Nama and Nokwanda Mtoto. Nosisana and I have a particularly trusting, close relationship. She is Xhosa-speaking and deeply connected to her ancestors and traditional values, while at the same time living in the modern, urban world. She acts as my guide and mentor, and together we learn from each other. There is mutual respect and trust; we have had to go through some difficult times.

The most intense of these was our naïve attempt at setting up a community resource for mothers and their infants in a renovated shipping container. Structurally altered containers are a frequent sight in the township—they act as telephone houses, meeting places, offices. We bought one from a woman, called by her clan name of Magadebe, who was running a crèche—she had a container that was not in use and we thought it appropriate to be situated near a place designated for the care of handicapped children. The money used had come as a gift from my family abroad, and in our trust of Magadebe, we did not ask for a receipt. Initially all went well. After we had a nighttime burglary, we appointed a night guard and paid him as well as Magadebe a monthly sum, besides paying the municipal rates for using this piece of land. My daughter and her school friends painted the container with bright flowers. We had a colorful inaugural ceremony. We used the container as our office once a week, and during other times it was used by other organizations that wanted to inform mothers about various issues—such as the safe use of paraffin. It seemed ideal. We called it the Mdlezana Centre—using an indigenous word for the unity between mother and infant.

However, gradually it became clear to us that Magadebe was a woman with trickster traits who was exploiting our goodwill. She told people that the container was hers and denied that we had paid a large sum for it. Other unpleasant, plainly untruthful allegations were made, such as that we were withholding from the community funds we were thought to have. We felt increasingly fearful and vulnerable, so much so that one of the women who worked with us and who lived nearby started having bad dreams and started fearing bewitchment. After her house was gutted by fire in December 1998, I decided it was time to move. The feeling of paranoia that was evoked was real and came from deep layers of the unconscious, plus of course very real outer danger. Through all this, Nosisana and I worked as a team. We understood Magadebe to be greedy and exercising a sense of entitlement, and that she was prepared to tell lies in order to obtain whatever money and material possessions she could. The notion of bewitchment, though foreign to me, became a concept that needed to be taken seriously, because it could have been a real threat to life.

When I told the head of the Department of Psychiatry at the university, he advised me not to go into the area for the time being. Nosisana, who does not live in Khayelitsha, shared this view. In January 1999 she went back in alone to feel out the atmosphere. It was only when she reported to me that everything seemed to be fine that I returned. We decided the best way forward was to continue our work in one of the official well-baby clinics where infants are brought for weighing and immunization. These are mainly staffed by nursing sisters. We eventually settled down in a clinic called Empilisweni, meaning "good health." This was situated in a subsection of Khayelitsha called Harare. This place felt safe, protected by the community and larger municipal structures and, above all, staffed by nurses who were professionals and cared deeply for their people. As part of the development of infrastructure in the townships in general, Khayelitsha also obtained new buildings for clinics. We have since moved to such a new building in Kuyasa, together with the same clinic, and continue our regular visits.

Looking at this process from a deeper perspective, several issues arise. Often I asked myself why I continued to want to work in this area. According to many white people living in Cape Town, going into the township in the first place was asking for trouble. I had heard this often enough. When I was then confronted with all these difficulties, the fears and predictions of unrealistic idealism seemed to be confirmed. The opinion was that our western values—of right and wrong, of boundaries between professional life and personal life, between the individual and collective—were not compatible in a community where seemingly other values, other rules pertained.

Why Continue?

What continued to motivate me on a conscious level were several factors: I regarded the preceding view as pejorative, one that was of the stereotyping kind reminiscent of the past. Cultural differences certainly do exist; the interaction with others, the dance one has with them, is in my experience much more complex, more differentiated than the western styles to which I am accustomed. Much more power lies in community relationships, in the interconnectedness between the people, than in the individualistic society of Europe and North America. What we experienced with Magadebe was an unfortunate incident, one we could have had in any society where there was so much poverty and deprivation.

Then there were the people I had come to know and respect—Nosisana as well as nursing staff and the mothers with their babies. They had become an integral and essential part of my life. I could not imagine being without them. At another level there was the wish to connect with the African culture, to be enriched and learn from age-old traditions, particularly those of ancestor reverence and the sharing spirit of *ubuntu* (discussed in chapter 6). In part this is making up for lost time—in the first half of my life I was prevented from engaging with African people on this level because of the political situation in the country and my own lack of awareness of what was happening. It is of course also about guilt and reparation, but there is more to it. In my European-ness I have lost my own connection to my ancestors, to a deeper universal rootedness. The separation anxiety that is so prevalent with western mothers and their babies seems to be almost nonexistent in traditional African culture. It is my impression that this might have to do with that linking to the clan and to the ancestors that is present for every individual from the very beginning of life. An individual person is part of a much larger whole—this notion is profoundly reassuring and accounts for the sense of equanimity that I come across, time and again. This is not resignation or depression, but a knowing of a greater order in which the individual is embedded.

I am mindful of the danger of romanticizing the other culture, of stereotyping and generalizing in an idealizing way. I do however have to stand by my very real experience over many years, namely that there is a special composure and acceptance among the black African people with whom I have come into contact; a sense of harmony that comes out of the knowing that one is part of a whole, a knowing deeply embedded in the collective psyche. This is of course not to deny or minimize the personal conflict, pain, and deprivation that exist in daily life. But it is humbling to be able to witness the life of so many brave parents and their children and to be able to help some of them. This is the reason for continuing.

CHAPTER 2

And What about the Infant?

When the Jungian analyst Mara Sidoli visited Cape Town in 1992 she presented a tape of an infant observation done by one of her students in the United States. The baby's name was Susan. During one scene on the tape her father is heard saying lovingly and repeatedly: "It's all about the mouth." This was fascinating—fascinating because a senior analyst paid such careful attention to little Susan; fascinating to become aware of the potential there resided within this small being; and fascinating because Susan was the living proof of psychoanalytic theory. Baby Susan was in a sense the beginning of clinical and research work with infants in South Africa. She gave the inspiration to inquire more deeply about early development and to engage psychotherapeutically with the child right from the beginning of life.

Complicating matters, clinicians in South Africa face the formidable task and challenge of reaching out to fellow citizens who are underprivileged and are often different and, sadly enough, alien to the practitioner in language and culture. Because of the country's political past, the effects of suspicion, prejudice, and lack of knowledge make reaching out to others often fraught and painful. Misunderstandings and indeed misdiagnoses are not uncommon (Swartz 1998).

Focusing on infants and paying attention to them, much like Mara

Sidoli did with baby Susan, made it possible to start at the beginning; to start with the simplest element and observe the tiniest movement. Sharing these observations provided an immediate link with the mother, who, like any mother, was delighted that someone was seeing her baby. Thus it was through the infant that we found a point of entry into a community, its hardships, its strength, and its culture. Jung's phrase "smaller than small yet bigger than big" (Jung 1959, 158) finds real application here and finds expression in various ways throughout this contribution. Through the baby a bridge is formed; in fact, the baby's very existence depends on bridges being formed.

Babies are equipped with attributes that result in their being a powerful motivating factor toward such bridge building—provided one is open to seeing and taking in. This seeing occurs at different levels:

1. Knowing about the abilities babies are born with—how they come into this world, hardwired to connect to other human beings, hardwired to make sense of the world around them.

2. Understanding their communication—talking to infants and allowing them to talk to us.

3. Allowing oneself to feel with the infant—to have empathy at a deep, preverbal, emotional level.

4. Allowing oneself to be moved by what the infant symbolizes: wholeness, hope, future; but also allowing oneself to enter into the dark space of the abandoned child, the helpless child.

The thrust of this chapter is to describe infants and the effect they have on those around them on these four levels: moving from the outer, observable, and more objectively scientific to the deeper affective and symbolic levels.

1. The Infant's Abilities

Human beings are multifaceted because of the complexity of our brain interconnections. These interconnections in turn are dependent on experience, most importantly experiences with important others (Perry et al. 1995; Schore 2001). It is not only biology that matters; the

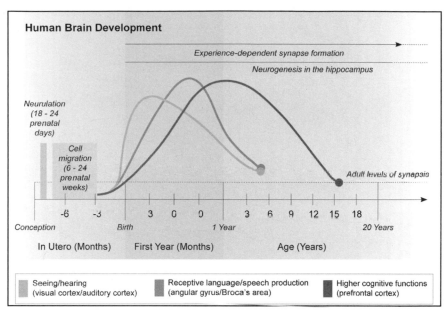

Adapted from R. A. Thompson and C. A. Nelson, 2001, "Developmental Science and the Media: Early Brain Development" (Am. Psychol. 56: 5–15).

quality of the environment significantly influences the development of the brain. From pregnancy through the second year of life the brain is in a critical period of accelerated growth (Schore 2002), one developmental event building on the other. Small perturbations at this sensitive stage could have long-term effects on the brain's structural and functional capacity (Grantham-McGregor et al. 2007).

Alessandra Piontelli (Piontelli 1992) conducted infant observation via the ultrasound scanner on fetuses in the womb. She found "a remarkable consistency in behaviour before and after birth" (23) and concluded that the links to prenatal patterns were not severed at birth (236). The interplay between nature and nurture thus begins much earlier than is usually thought, and certain prenatal experiences may have an ongoing emotional effect on the child (1).

Taking a perspective from the other side, Erich Neumann (1973) hypothesized that the first year of life could be regarded as an "extra-

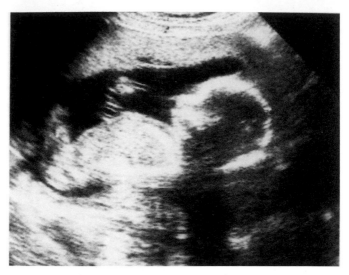

Ultrasound of fetus at about sixteen weeks gestation.

uterine" embryonic phase: the infant comes into this world physically immature and vulnerable, needing at least another nine to twelve months to reach some degree of bodily competence and independence. The absolute dependence (Winnicott 1990) of the child on a primary caregiver places the child in a context of human relationships from the very start. It may be this fact that contributes to making us human beings so interesting and so complex.

What do babies bring with them that enables them to make optimal use of the experiences available to them and that lays the foundation for building bridges toward the other? We take the world in through our senses—we smell, taste, feel, hear, and see—and in this way we learn. The fetal and newborn brain is not blank—it is well equipped and very active, ready to learn. Various sensory modalities have been shown to be present and functioning from about twenty weeks of gestation onward (Lagercrantz and Changeux 2009).

The fetus freely swims about in the amniotic fluid, able to smell this and later, after birth, recognize it as familiar (Marlier et al. 1998). Movements become restricted as the pregnancy progresses, but the full repertoire of activity seen in the newborn is already present (Kurjak et al.

2004) long before. We could imagine the fetus touching the wall of the womb—perhaps even intentionally going there to feel it again.

We can also imagine the sounds that surround a fetus. The background noise is low frequency, consisting of maternal abdominal gurgles and heartbeat. Voices, especially the mother's voice, are of a different order. Fetuses differentiate between the low frequency sounds and the higher pitched human voices. The mother's voice has particular significance as it is transmitted in two ways: via air conduction as well as bone conduction—it thus comes across better than any of the other external voices. And fetuses remain interested in the mother's voice and do not attenuate to it so readily (Lecanuet 1996). They also prefer to hear their mother tongue spoken (Kisilevsky et al. 2009).

These are measurable scientific findings, but we need to go deeper, something psychoanalyst Suzanne Maiello has done. On the basis of her analytic understanding from working with young children and adults as well as from her infant observation studies, she makes the following hypothesis: she suggests that the sound of the mother's voice prenatally is significant; the fact that it is there not continuously, but alternating with silence, could give the child the proto-experience of absence and presence. She has termed the mother's voice the "sound object" and postulates that this may constitute the precursor to the maternal inner object (Maiello 1995). She sensitizes us to the meaning of sound, emphasizing the emotional quality that is expressed at a sound-level (Maiello 1997), something that remains with us throughout life.

Vision is the one sensory modality that comes into play only after birth. While visual acuity in infants is poor relative to that of adults (Schwarzer and Leder 2003), newborn infants can process complex visual stimuli; they have a constitutional bias ensuring that they fixate on faces (Johnson 2005); even directly after birth most babies open their eyes (Lamberg 1981); they look at the face and want to establish direct eye contact, preferably with the mother. The wish to communicate with the other is thus there from the very beginning, even if this is not yet conscious, not yet verbal. The neural pathways that play a role in face detection and preferential looking are located at a subcortical level (Johnson 2005)—that is, they do not yet involve the higher brain functions active when the person is fully conscious and aware.

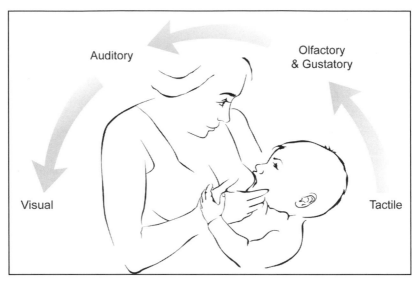

Nursing a baby provides a clear illustration of the linking of sensory inputs.

The point in time when consciousness fully emerges remains a puzzle confronting the scientific world—a wide neural network has to mature before a person can have the sensory awareness of the body, the self, and the world (Lagercrantz and Changeux 2009). However, the beginnings of basic consciousness can be seen in newborn infants; what happens at a lower, subcortical level is already remarkable, and it is this that lays the groundwork, the basis for full consciousness to emerge.

The sensory systems function and are ready to take in the world—not only to take it in directly but to make connections across the different modalities. For example, Meltzoff and Borton in 1979 showed how twenty-nine-day-old infants could recognize which of two visually perceived shapes matched one they had previously explored only tactually (Meltzoff and Borton 1979). The correspondence in their minds between touch and vision was present and accurate, and this kind of accuracy and fluency has been demonstrated in the other sensory modalities too. The first six weeks of life are the time when the infant is actively forming connections in a cross-modal manner, and this lays the basis for a sense of "core self" that will remain for the rest of the child's life (Stern 1985).

With these innate abilities the child enters the world—into the do-main of the mother and of being mothered. Jacoby (1999) calls this inheritance "archetypal." Perhaps it would be more accurate to name these attributes genetic predispositions; they do after all appear in some form in other animals too. What may be termed archetypal are the ways in which the human infant is born with a pre-figuration, with a prototype in mind, which prompts the infant to seek that pat-terning in the other and thus lay the foundation for being in relation-ship with another human being.

In his critical review of Jung's *Archetypes and the Collective Uncon-scious* R. F. Hobson makes the important point that the term *arche-type* is being used too loosely, including by Jung himself, and raises the question "whether it is appropriate to refer to archetypes by such names as mother, child, trickster, or even rebirth. These names imply a particular matter of content, and it might be that we shall have to evolve abstract formal methods of representation such as are used in mathematics or mathematical logic" (Hobson 1961, 166).

Many years later Jean Knox reexamined the concept of arche-types in the light of developmental research in infants (Knox 2003) and took up (possibly inadvertently) what Hobson suggests. She challenges the established definition of archetypes as being meta-physical entities; she contends that there is no such thing as innate knowledge of images or themes—knowledge such as this would imply the activation of higher, neocortical functions which are not fully developed in the first years of life. Archetypes do not come to us in the form of myths or images, nor are they carried thus within our genetic makeup—these are constellated through time in inter-action with the environment. What is inherited is the predisposition at a subcortical level to perceive image schemas—for example, the archetype of the great mother may be nothing more than a small circle being contained by a larger circle. What happens later to this schema is influenced by the family, the society, and the culture with-in which the child is embedded. Only then does it become filled in with images and myths of "the great mother" and the "divine child," and these might not exist in every culture. What is in the collective unconscious is our human predisposition to orient ourselves from

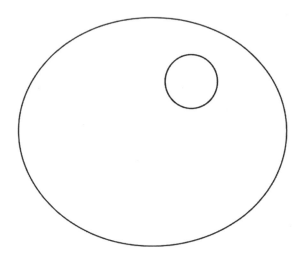

Image schema of the small contained within the large, according to Knox (2003).

the very beginning of life to certain simple patterns and that these patterns coincide with and are amplified by experiences that the environment provides.

2. Communicating with Infants

The extraordinary capacities of very young infants are appreciated by most mothers—they could have told us what is painstakingly being proven scientifically. They know that their infants can hear and see, can recognize them, and they know that infants can talk to them; in the past this knowing has mostly been perceived to be parental doting and was perhaps sometimes ascribed to loving imagination. However, once there is proof from a laboratory, as has happened over the past two decades, this innate knowledge assumes a different meaning—infants have now become the objects of intense research. There is a burgeoning fund of new knowledge; from a clinical perspective, the infants and their relationships have become the new patient.

As I have described, the infant arrives in this world fully geared to making connections. The different sensory modalities connect with one another, and the sense of self slowly emerges. At the age of about two months, a shift is seen in the way the infants behave and relate to changes. They become more attentive, more focused on people. The time from two to six months has been described as the "most exclusively social period of life" (Stern 1985, 72). Infants at this age compel one to interact with them—if only we were to look and see, we would not be able to walk away without a smile, without a wink or a coo.

And so it is thus predisposed that exactly this kind of socializing is needed for the brain to develop. Face-to-face interaction is the most potent of growth stimulator for brain cells; it induces the production of neurotrophins, which in turn promote the formation of neuronal connections (Schore 2001). Of course this interaction has to be positive and attuned to the infant's threshold for stimulation. An intrusive, looming face, a loud voice, and sudden, jerky movements are experienced as threatening and disorganizing (David and Lyons-Ruth 2005) and could have the opposite effect. Early relational trauma is neurotoxic and can lead to cell death, which in turn can ultimately result in alteration in the brain's architecture (Schore 2002).

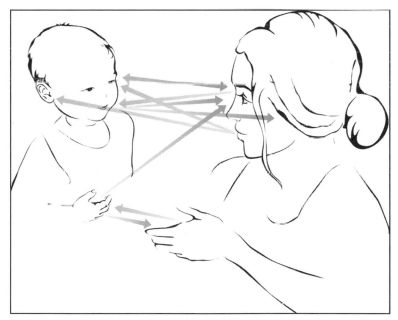

Face-to-face interaction stimulates brain growth.

These two findings, namely that positive interaction stimulates brain growth and that traumatic interactions can be damaging to brain structure, place an enormous responsibility on the shoulders of clinicians, policy makers, and indeed politicians. We cannot but agree with the observation that "preservation of the mental health of infants is the key to the prevention of mental disorder throughout the lifespan" (Fonagy 1998, 126). If the infant is the patient, the one who suffers, how is one to engage when on the face of it, no mutual conversation is possible? Does the "talking cure" have a place?

Psychoanalyst Johan Norman suggests in a 1997 paper an answer that could serve as a model. His "To Talk with Infants: The Relationship between Baby and Analyst as a Port of Entry into the Mother-and-Baby-Relationship" is provocative in that he talks with six-month-old baby Lisa in much the same way as he would do with any adult or older child analysand (in Norman 2001). Lisa's mother had suffered from a depression that required hospitalization when Lisa was two months old. The mother was now concerned that Lisa was not meeting her eye, and she felt rejected by her daughter.

When Norman saw mother and child for the first time he was perturbed by the distance between them and by the emergency that this constituted—baby Lisa needed help now, and mother's depression could still last a long time. He describes how he simply turned to Lisa and spoke to her, saying that they would try together to understand what it was that disturbed them both so much. When Lisa began to whimper, he would notice his counter-transference and talk about the pain and fear he felt. He tried to find words for the images that were coming up for him, and it was as though this induced Lisa to try to connect with her mother. Stormy and painful sessions followed, but through the containment of the presence and words of the analyst, mother and baby weathered the sessions and were able to establish a relationship.

What is evident from this case is that Lisa was able to form a relationship with the analyst that was distinct and different from her relationship with her mother. Also evident is that Lisa could find containment in the words spoken—not the literal meaning of the words but the way in which they were communicated. Sincerity and authenticity are vital. The therapist's whole being has to be involved when speaking with an infant; there can be no disjunction between gesture, tone of voice, and content of what is said.

The second case I want to bring is from my clinic and is different in terms of the circumstances and setting, but the main thrust of talking and of bestowing personhood onto the baby is similar (Berg 2002a). Kwanga was five months old when he was referred to the clinic. His mother was twenty-one years old. His recent failure to thrive was of concern—two months before there had been a marked drop in his weight. Kwanga had had gastroenteritis but had not picked up his weight since then, although the symptoms had ceased.

On history taking, it emerged that he was mother's first child. His maternal grandmother was living in the Eastern Cape, while his young mother was "drifting from aunt to aunt," as she had no fixed abode in Khayelitsha. The father of the child was not really present, and she was entirely dependent on the aunts. She stopped breastfeeding when Kwanga was one month old, because the baby "did not want to." It seems that the bottle feeding and the gastroenteritis contributed to the drop in weight. The mother denied any other problems, saying she loved her baby and that she herself was eating and sleeping well. These few facts we elicited with some difficulty.

We observed that this young mother was well dressed, as was her baby. She would give him a pacifier when he cried (this is a rare habit; usually in Khayelitsha the breast is given for comfort). Kwanga was quite a thin child. His mother was cut off from him and avoided eye contact with the interviewers and with her baby. I felt that her eyes were "drifting," like she was with her life. The team had a sense of hopelessness when they heard this story and when they saw the non-interaction and wondered what could be done. Because the mother denied any negative feelings, it seemed pointless to be empathetic.

After a while my co-worker Nosisana took Kwanga, put him on her lap, and talked to him. He needed to be coaxed to respond, but eventually he did so with a smile and physical movements. His mother did not take any delight in this and looked away. However, when her problems were addressed, she did look at Nosisana more steadily. I asked that Kwanga be turned to look at his mother, but he avoided her—he rather looked at us. He was returned to his mother, and now for the first time she held him facing her and smiled at him, and it appeared that he met her gaze. His mother was given a pamphlet explaining the importance of interacting with the baby.

The baby's failure to thrive was diagnosed as deriving from depression and deprivation in his mother. We hypothesized that the early weaning occurred because there was no older mothering figure to help this young woman. She was asked to return in two weeks. By the second visit Kwanga's weight had increased, and when Nosisana approached him, he cried, indicating that he had now attached to his mother. He was more responsive to her and more alive. His mother had a "lighter" feel about her and she was interacting with him face to face. She was still living with an aunt, but the relationship with the boyfriend seemed to have stabilized. She spontaneously said that Kwanga looked like his father. This was an important acknowledgement in that the feelings belonging to the father can so easily be displaced onto the baby. This young woman felt more positive toward her boyfriend, and this in turn may have enabled her to have the same feelings toward her infant son.

This case illustrates how even in dire circumstances where poverty and family disconnectedness are so prevalent, and where official social support is so limited, and where the mother seems unreachable and closed off, turning to the infant can result in bringing new life into the situation. The baby was spoken to, he responded to us, and the mother saw this. Something seemed to have changed for her, enabling her to take her baby and do the same for him. His weight gain and his attachment to her were evident during the subsequent visit.

The harder the struggle for physical existence is, the more basic and simpler everything seems to become. In psychotherapeutic interventions, a regular twice-weekly talking session is neither possible nor appropriate. However, the essence of the interaction remains the same whether in Stockholm or in a township in Cape Town: seeing the infant and her or his distress, taking this seriously, and communicating this to the infant. All infants need to be recognized as persons who are eager to communicate.

3. Allowing Oneself to Feel with the Infant

It is not enough simply to see the infants and then talk to them—that will not work, as more than seeing and talking is needed. The infant evokes in us deep feelings, and it is with these that we need to respond to the infant—otherwise there would be no authenticity, no depth, and babies are quick to pick this up. Selma Fraiberg and her team were the first clinicians to work directly with parents and their infants, in the 1970s. They were acutely aware of their counter-transference reactions engendered by this work and stated: "No case report can ever do justice to the feelings of the therapist who works with infants and their parents" (Shapiro et al. 1976, 145). In the case Fraiberg described, clinicians felt anger toward the schoolgirl mother who was starving her baby; in Johan Norman's description of Lisa he felt urgency and desperation at the lack of movement in the mother; with Kwanga we felt hopelessness and helplessness. In all there is a conscious and unconscious identification with the infant: the vulnerable being who is so absolutely dependent on the caregiver who is not doing what nature intended. Why has it taken humanity so long to discover the infant? And why do infants and young children continue to bear the brunt in warfare and domestic violence? Perhaps we as adults do not dare to look at the infant in ourselves.

Infants are physically vulnerable and weak, and they cannot speak; they thus serve as ideal recipients of projections. Nowhere is this seen more starkly than in the history of childhood. During antiquity the killing of both legitimate and illegitimate children was a regular practice (deMause 1974). Two theories are put forward as to why this could have been so: first, that the infant is used as a vehicle for projection of unwanted contents of the adults' unconscious—"projective reaction"; and second, that the child is treated as a substitute for an adult figure in the parent's life—what deMause calls "reversal reaction."

However, if we start to think about infants as full human beings from the very beginning, who have abilities that allow them to see, hear, and feel in their own right, then the projection and reversal reactions are challenged. If we regard the infant as subject, not as object, we enter another realm of relating and doing psychotherapy (Salo

2007). We can no longer afford to hide behind defensive reactions such as "they are too young to notice." The denial has to give way to acknowledgment—and it is a painful, indeed an excruciating acknowledgment. It confronts us with our own beginnings, and we have to imagine what it could be like to be that infant whose mother is not available, who fails time and again to respond appropriately to his needs. From an adult's perception such a breach may not be that dire; but from the baby's point of view this maternal failure is experienced as catastrophic (Baradon 2005). We have to use our imagination, as Jan Wiener so clearly invites us to do when working with countertransference (Wiener 2009). In the case of infant psychotherapy it is about finding the words for what we feel that could link to what we imagine the baby might feel.

Ann Morgan, the well-known Australian infant therapist, talks of "truthfulness" as being important—to be aware of one's own thinking, aware of the infant's thinking and working toward understanding it, no matter how young the infant (Morgan 2007, 16). She further states that people who work with babies have to allow themselves to feel and to be with the baby. The actual verbal response matters less than the truthfulness of it; and it can only be truthful if we allow ourselves to feel with and for the baby.

Once we have understood and integrated the fact of infants as sentient beings, we cannot remain aloof and dispassionate: there is something compelling that draws us into their world, and into what they represent—indeed, it becomes an issue of human rights. Human dignity and justice are not the prerogatives strictly of verbal adults—they extend to the helpless and wordless; in fact, these vulnerable people require human rights possibly more than anyone else. The feelings evoked in us with infants go beyond the personal. If there is a universal human theme that connects us all, it is the way in which we all began this life.

4. Allowing Oneself to Be Moved
by What the Infant Symbolizes

Jung contends that the child archetype serves as an excellent example of his concept of the archetype; he proceeds to mention several aspects that are contained in the child motif (Jung 1959). These motifs, however, could be seen as already advanced developments of the core image, elaborations of the *archetype-an-sich,* the essential structure of the archetype. If Jean Knox's view is followed, then the archetypal schema from which the child motif is formed is the simple image of the small circle embedded in the larger one. Free association on this plain configuration could lead to many thoughts and pictures, but even if one stays close to this simple image of the small within the big, several questions arise. Is the small contained or is it engulfed? Is it floating in empty space within the circle, or is it held gently in place? Will it be able to grow in size, or will it be restricted and kept little?

The infant or child symbolizes that which is tiny, vulnerable, and dependent but also that which has the potential to change and grow. A baby is new, filled with hope and possibilities. The infant engenders in those who dare to look and listen a complex set of emotions. Most adults know children—our own, or those in our neighborhoods; we have taken care of them or have seen them grow up. The subject matter is close to home. But the feelings evoked when infancy and childhood are discussed point to something deeper emerging. The responses are often intense and often seem to bypass rational thinking. Two sets of emotions are commonly stirred up: a sense of wonder and excitement and sadness or guilt.

The reason for these intense emotions is that infants and children connect us with our personal history as well as our collective human history: We all were babes in the arms of someone at some time past. If we were to let go of our defenses of denial and rationalization, we could get in touch with what it feels like to be helpless and utterly dependent. We feel sad for ourselves, for our inner child who has invariably suffered in not having needs met. Impingements, misattunements, misunderstandings in early life occur for all of us; it is part of our human condition. If repeated and if they are traumatic, they can leave lasting imprints on our psyches. The literal abandonment of the child is a tragic reality that does occur and for which no excuse or higher meaning can be found. Many parents struggle with guilt and with questions of whether they did what they should not have done.

Jung tends to gloss over the actual child who really does get abandoned—perhaps this is too close to home and he could not attend to this aspect of reality. We know his mother left him for several months when he was an infant, as she had to be hospitalized for depression (Jung 1963). His sense of early abandonment must have been profound, and he was consequently more at ease talking about the child in a symbolic sense. Therapists, however, ought to know that the real, lived childhood experience of a patient should not be skipped over in order to get to the symbolic child—the work is not done if pain and sadness are avoided; and the symbolic child should not be used defensively.

But once the personal feelings have been dealt with, there is a very real place for looking at the symbol of the child. For example, metaphoric abandonment is necessary in order for children to find their own strength and be able to detach from their origins, as Jung has stated. To be *"all alone in the world"* (Jung 1959, 169) is a prerequisite to going beyond what one already is, going beyond present day consciousness. Only in this way can we grow up and individuate.

And this is where the child could be a symbol that bridges two poles: from being small and all alone in the world to manifesting that which is possible, to realizing that which is new. And this is where the thrill, the hope comes in when dealing with the subject of infancy. Every baby born is a fresh beginning—most parents all over the world are in awe of this event: this new human being coming into life is something that is out of everyday life, something that is extraordinary. This child embodies hope: hope that his or her life will be good, will be better than that of the parents; hope that this human being will make the world a better place—the list of hopes and possibilities is long.

A quote from Jung captures the essence:

The archetype of the child . . . expresses man's wholeness. The "child" is all that is abandoned and exposed and at the same time divinely powerful; the insignificant, dubious beginning, and the triumphal end. The "eternal child" in man is an indescribable experience, an incongruity, a handicap, and a divine prerogative: an imponderable that determines the ultimate worth or worthlessness of a personality. (Jung 1959, 179)

Within the infant there is as yet no persona, there is no false self, no trickery or manipulations; a baby is a baby and nothing more and nothing less. An infant speaks to us and it does not matter whether skin color is black, brown, or white, and it does not matter whether the baby is a boy or a girl—we have to respond. Infants thus help us, indeed they require us, to transcend the boundaries of race and gender.

The Baby as Bridge

Entry into a black community that had been kept separate from the white population, a community whose language and culture I consequently experienced as foreign, was made possible. The baby provided a bridge to the other: human infants are the same all over the world, their needs are the same, and they impel us to connect with them, and that connection can only come through an honest encounter, an authentic communication. In a sense the infant stands in the middle of the bridge, beckoning us from both sides—and demanding of us to be real. We have to know ourselves, we have to get beyond our personas, our prejudices, when we face a little person—and once that step is taken, the other steps follow: the communication with the mother, the understanding of her world with all the complexity of our particular political history, her language and culture, and her socioeconomic hardship.

Children are bridges to our self and to the other. Nietzsche's Zarathustra had withdrawn into the mountains, into his cave. He was progressively feeling more and more pain, as he had nowhere to go with all he wanted to give. What to do next was revealed to him in a dream:

a child appeared with a mirror and instructed him to look at himself (Nietzsche 1964, 87). What he saw there frightened him, and he knew he had to go back into the world and give his love and wisdom to the people.

The insight that he could no longer be by himself came to him through a child—Zarathustra could not ignore this; neither can we. Children compel us to action. Among all the many issues that Nelson Mandela has addressed, this one has remained close to his heart: "There can be no keener revelation of a society's soul than the way in which it treats its children" (in Asmal et al. 2003, 421).

CHAPTER 3

The Baby's Name Was
Not Understood

A CASE OF FAILED AND POSSIBLY SUCCESSFUL
MOTHER-INFANT PSYCHOTHERAPY

The story of this little boy and his mother is one that has not left me: through them I was compelled to obtain deeper knowledge of a particular African culture. What had been born out of a sense of a clinical duty has become a source of great wisdom. The factual account of this dyad is given. The mother granted permission for the story to be shared, and for the names to be used, as she said: "It is the truth, not lies, and it should be told." The story has been told and written up before, and it is one that has been memorable to those who have heard and read about it (Berg 2003a).

The clinical picture as it unfolded is described here again and two formulations are given: one in terms of the clinical and psychodynamic model, the other in terms of the cultural context of this mother and her baby. This case demonstrates the importance of bearing in mind that medically and psychoanalytically, a viewpoint deriving from a western perspective may not be universally applicable. There should be awareness of the cultural bias and of the consequent limitations this imposes. All efforts should be made to be truly mindful of the other and to be open to taking a different viewpoint.

Athi's Beginning

Athi was born in a maternity hospital in Cape Town in April 1995. He was his twenty-five-year-old mother's second child. She was married and had a young daughter. Athi was a premature baby of thirty-four weeks gestation and required a period of hospital care. He was transferred to a Premature Unit, from which he was discharged just before he was one month old. Throughout this time his mother, Nosakhele, had managed to breastfeed him.

Twenty-four hours after discharge, his mother brought him back to the hospital because of breathing problems. On closer examination it became evident that he had sustained third-degree burns in his mouth and of his upper throat. He was transferred to the Red Cross War Memorial Children's Hospital in Cape Town, a tertiary, academic hospital dedicated to the care of children. The doctors resuscitating him, world experts in burn surgery, doubted their heroic efforts would succeed and wondered

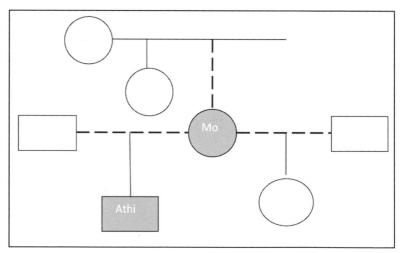

A genogram of Athi depicts some of the baby's family context.

whether the damage to his mouth was too severe to allow for any quality of life in the future. However, they persisted; he was fitted with a tracheostomy for breathing, and a gastrostomy for feeding purposes.

When Athi was three months old, an infant mental health consultation was requested by the social worker in the hospital ward. There was concern about how and into whose care he should be discharged. His mother had moved into the hospital and had taken care of him throughout this period. She had been staying with her husband and his family, but he had left her. Her older daughter had gone back to the Eastern Cape. A few days before the consultation request, the mother had disclosed to a social worker from the community, who was able to speak her language, that she had wanted to kill her baby—this was the first time she had shown emotions and had volunteered information. It was at this delicate point that I became involved, having just started the Infant Mental Health Service. This was the first official referral received by the service.

On history taking, the following emerged: prior to Athi's conception Nosakhele, a married woman, went to visit her ailing mother in the Eastern Cape—a former "homeland" known for its high levels of unemployment and poverty. While there, she needed money to help her take care of her mother. A married man offered to pay her for a sexual favor—this she did, and Athi was conceived. When the man heard about it, he distanced himself from Nosakhele and the pregnancy. She returned home to her husband and his family and gave birth to the baby. This was as much as we knew and understood at the time.

I visited Athi in the ward and my observations were:

He is a small baby, lying prone in his bed, sleeping. He has a tracheostomy and thus his crying cannot be heard. He did not fully wake while I was there—but opened his eyes slightly, pulling his face as if crying; no movement of arms or legs. His mother is a young, sad looking woman who smiled briefly when I introduced myself via an interpreter. She went about her job of feeding him through the tube in a quiet, efficient way—I was out of the ward for 5 minutes, and when I returned she had finished. She cleaned his bedside table and brought his washing which she was going to fold or sort out. She had covered her baby, but did not hold him. He seemed to have been sleeping throughout.

My assessment at the time was as follows:

> This young mother finds herself in an impossible situation. Having a child from another married man, while she herself is married, must be one of the most profound transgressions within her cultural setting. That she should have become depressed and have impulses to get rid of her baby is a very real possibility. Her worst fears have probably realized themselves now in that she has been abandoned.
>
> While she is in hospital and is receiving care herself, she is able to be a good mother. The question is how she will cope on discharge. A structure and containment for both mother and baby will have to be set in place before discharge can even be considered. She also needs an ongoing supportive relationship.

A week later I noted that while mother was caring and gentle with Athi, there was little contact between them. On a subsequent visit I observed that Athi had his head to the side and stared ahead of him. His eyes were big and bright and looked intelligent. After some effort on my part to get into his visual field, he eventually focused on me and seemed to look at my face. Mother's handling of him was methodical and careful, but she did not once speak to him nor try to look into his eyes. Athi likewise made no effort to look at his mother. When I said good-bye to him and his mother, "He looked at me, frowning. I told him to look at his mother and I aligned their gazes, telling him that I was not his mother and showing him his mother. His mother laughed, but seemed to understand what I was saying." My impression at that visit was that Athi's interest in the world could be enhanced, if more attention were to be paid to his eye contact and facial movements. However, I was concerned about an autistic defense developing should this gap between him and his mother not be addressed.

It was considered that the best way to proceed was for his mother to be encouraged through empathetic explanation and role modeling to focus on him more. A clinical social work colleague, who could speak with mother in her own language, was requested to do weekly sessions with mother and infant. The social worker's input seemed to have had positive effects in that the interactions between mother and Athi became more spontaneous; she would sing to him, he would turn to her and the occupational therapist could not work with him now without mother being present. Athi was at this stage six months old.

On the outer level, the mother seemed to have been reunited with her husband's family over weekends, but as nothing had been said to her about Athi, she did not want to go there with him. Discharge was discussed, a discharge date was set, and alternative accommodation was sought. However, soon thereafter he developed pneumonia and had to remain in the hospital—his mother looked visibly upset and expressed disappointment at this setback. He gradually improved and another discharge date was set.

One week later Athi had collapsed. It was inexplicable medically, and the doctors were puzzled by these two sudden attacks. A perceptive junior doctor sent blood for toxicology screening and the results were shocking: they revealed that Athi had been poisoned with organic phosphate. His mother had been the only one to feed and care for him, and there was no doubt that she had done this, probably on two occasions. The police were called, and she was immediately apprehended, charged, and imprisoned.

An emotional period followed in the ward and the hospital. Nosakhele had moved from being the mother who had worked hard to become "good enough," and whom everybody liked, to someone who was so evil that she wanted to kill her baby. As his mother had been banished, Athi became everyone's baby. The press got hold of the story, which made headlines. Offers to adopt Athi came from strangers. The chief nurse of the ward took a special interest in him, one that remains to date.

I was subpoenaed to court and had to testify to the damage that the mother had done to Athi—physically and emotionally. When I also wanted to explain mother's position, I was angrily stopped by the prosecutor, who told me very firmly that I was there to represent the baby only. By this time I had a better understanding of what Nosakhele was trying to tell us, but my insight came too late.

As with most issues that pertain to human relationships, there are many facets, many different angles from which one can view happenings and interactions. And often, the way these are seen can have profound consequences. When one culture is looked at through the lens of another, these consequences can be particularly grave.

The Western Clinical Perspective

From a basic clinical, western perspective the thinking and the approach we followed cannot be faulted. The attachment relationship between mother and infant was disturbed because of family and individual psychopathology. The young woman had acted out of desperation, and the result was the conception of an illegitimate baby. This placed her in an untenable situation with her husband and parents-in-law. She acted out a second time by trying to do away with her child.

Infanticide is a phenomenon that has been recorded since the beginning of history (deMause 1974). Unwanted babies were regularly done away with. During the early 1800s in Europe, up to a third of infants were killed or abandoned by their parents (Wissow 1998). It has since steadily declined to about 9 per 100,000 live births during the early 1990s, being mostly seen as a symptom of postpartum depression (Almond 2009). What Nosakhele tried to do was horrific and was an attempted murder, but it has been described before—she is not the first mother to have been so despairing of her situation. However, what was unusual was the fact that she was neither psychotic nor suffering from a major depressive episode. There was no psychiatric disorder to be treated medically; the focus of management was on the infant and the attachment relationship. Athi's turning away from his mother and avoiding her gaze was of concern—something urgent had to be done about this in order to avoid an autistic defense of the self from becoming established.

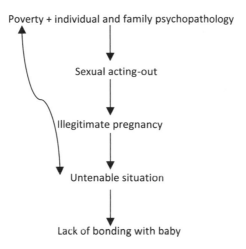

Poverty + individual and family psychopathology

Sexual acting-out

Illegitimate pregnancy

Untenable situation

Lack of bonding with baby

A psychodynamic formulation for Nosakele reflects some of the mother's difficulties.

What Was Not Seen

Had we looked more carefully and put the pieces of the puzzle together, the following should have alerted us to a more profound psychic process going on in this young woman than merely a nonattachment to her baby. First, she had mothered a child before—she knew what to do, as was clear from the confident manner in which she handled Athi. She would also naturally have made more contact with him—good mothers do this, no matter what their culture or language (Stern 2002). If they do not, there is something impeding them, but they do not need to be taught unless they are severely disturbed, which this mother was not.

Nosakhele was trying to tell us something through her nonverbal behavior of not looking at her child, and the professionals around her did not pick this up. I even made the comment in one of my reports: "Although mother may be well taught by now as far as the physical caring of her baby is concerned, the emotional bonding process has only just begun, if at all." However, I did not reflect on my own observations more deeply.

Second, we had not linked the fact that the improvement in her relationship with Athi coincided with her return to her husband and his family and thus never inquired directly about this. Had she not hoped that they would accept her and her baby? Or had she already made a plan not to have her child discharged from the hospital? Or was she merely following what was said to her in order to please the therapist whom she liked? Our view, in retrospect, was a rather superficial one, and our treatment of strengthening the mother-infant relationship was well meant but did not take into account the cultural context of this dyad.

The Cultural "Lostness" of Athi and Nosakhele

The crucial insight, however, came when the meaning of his name was explained: the full name she had given him was Athenkosi, which means "we thank the ancestors." Once this became clear to me, a fuller picture emerged of Nosakhele's desperate situation, which we had not previously grasped. Nosakhele gave him this "deep" name, hoping that her husband and his family would accept the baby as theirs. This was a boy, a son whom she wanted to give to the family, to their clan, and ultimately to their ancestors. She had dared to wish that they would indeed thank the ancestors for this baby boy. But they did not do that; they did not accept the child, because they could work out that he was not their blood child, and blood ties are strong in African culture.

But not only did the family not accept Athi—there was an additional insult: Athi could not be introduced to his ancestors; he could thus not be accepted by them. This meant that he would not have been able to go through the rituals of childhood and adolescence (van der Vliet 1974). And this in turn would mean that he could never become a man in the true sense of the word. Given Nosakhele's traditional, rural background, a more profound sense of loss of identity can hardly be imagined. It amounted to a loss of personhood for both of them. With this prospect of literal banishment and the nonpersonhood of herself and her son, Nosakhele acted out in a desperate manner.

I felt enormous guilt when I saw her in the courtroom. While she did damage Athi, she did it from a fraught place, and we had failed her. She was not psychotic or even depressed in a major way; she was lost, cut off from her moorings, an individual without the tools

Athenkosi = we thank the Ancestors

BUT

Neither clan accepts the baby

↓

The Ancestors cannot be thanked

↓

Rituals cannot be performed

↓

Loss of personhood

Cultural formulation expresses problems not captured via standard clinical procedures.

or the means to stand by her individuality and the choices she had made. How lost she was becomes clearer through subsequent chapters. If only that had been understood earlier, if only the full meaning of Athi's name had been grasped, perhaps some of this devastation could have been prevented. Nosakhele was sentenced to twelve years' imprisonment, and Athi was placed in a children's home. His first language became Afrikaans, and he seemed completely cut off from his roots; a beautiful Xhosa boy, not at all in touch with his mother tongue, let alone his mother's customs. Could Nosakhele have chosen another cultural route out of her dilemma?

Cultural Alternatives That Also Were Not Possible

In many parts of Africa an illegitimate pregnancy, particularly if the mother is a teenager, is not necessarily regarded as a calamity. Being fertile and becoming a mother is what most of life is about for most young women. Marriage is obviously preferred, but if a conception should take place beforehand, there is a way in which the situation can be contained within the families: a ritual known as the *inhlawulo* takes place (Berg 2003a). This entails the family of the boy visiting the family of the girl, and a "confession" is made that the girl's childhood has been robbed through the actions of the boy. In order to repair the damages, a sum of money, or, in rural areas in the past, a cow or other animal, is given to the girl's family. This payment of damages goes a long way toward ensuring the goodwill of the family on the girl's side. It does not mean that the couple will get married; it is merely a recognition, an acknowledgement (Preston-Whyte and Zondi 1996). It does mean that for future traditional ceremonies, the child will at least know who his father is and can call on the paternal family to be present. If the *inhlawulo* does not take place, it could have negative consequences for the young mother and her child. For example, the mother of the girl may refuse to help out in looking after the baby—as she may feel angry toward and humiliated by the family of the boy. The maternal grandmother's involvement in child care is central, and if she rejects her daughter or her grandchild, the consequences for both can be grave.

It is clear that Nosakhele's situation was completely different from that of a single girl or woman becoming pregnant. She had crossed a boundary, committed an act that would be damned in all cultures. The only way open to her would have been to have given birth to the baby while remaining with her mother in the Eastern Cape, and then giving the child over to the care of his grandmother, and only thereafter returning to her husband and his family. If it were not mentioned or discussed, and if it were not broadly known in the community, this family might well have taken her back—as we had seen when she visited them on her own over weekends. Generally speaking, the capacity to forgive and move on is enormous in Africa, and possibly born out of necessity: life is too complicated and too hard to remain focused on past transgressions and difficulties. Unfortunately, this avenue was also closed for Nosakhele, as her mother was very ill and was in no state to look after a young child. Nosakhele could thus only appear at her husband's home without Athi—as soon as she brought him there the facts would be starkly exposed, and this would have been too much of a disgrace.

The question that should have been posed to her, immediately after she had given her newborn baby poison to drink was: Do you want your child? Would you want us to give him to a person who will look after him, thereby freeing you to continue with your life? Adoption is not generally practiced in its formal sense in traditional societies, so she might not have been aware of this legally accepted possibility. It seems wrong that a mother might want to give away her child. It seems so contrary to nature that it becomes unthinkable and unaskable. But since this experience, it is a question that I have come to ask with much more ease—if the tone is gentle, and if the attitude is one of empathy, mothers do not take this question amiss; in fact, they feel seen and they feel relieved, that what they are experiencing is shareable and understandable.

Five Years Later

Five years after the incident I went to visit the mother in prison, together with Nosisana Nama, my cultural mentor and interpreter. Nosakhele looked well, but it was clear that she had not had many visitors. She recognized me and said she had no bad feelings toward me. Together we were able to reconstruct the events. This was important to me, as I wanted to hear from her whether the hypotheses I had made in the meantime were valid. And this is the story, taken directly from my notes:

When she fell pregnant, no one knew by whom, she could not even tell her mother for whom she had been getting the money. Her mother had been ill, and her father had died 2 years before. She has one older sister who is married—she did not talk to her either.

When she returned to Cape Town she tried to make the pregnancy her husband's, but he was "too clever" and worked out that it could not have been so. She was scared of him and did not want to show him the baby. He never saw Athi as he was returned to hospital immediately after his discharge from the neonatal unit. On asking her about the meaning of the name, she said she liked "Athenkosi" but had not thought of its deeper meaning.

While she was at Red Cross Children's Hospital with Athi she felt very conflicted. She knew she had been forgiven for the first attempt on Athi's life, but she was very scared of going to her husband with the baby. She said she was not open with us, and she blames herself for this. She said she never wanted Athi; she rejected him from the beginning. When she was told by Tumi (the social worker) what to do with Athi and encouraged to bond with him, she felt very bad, because inside she could not do this. She also felt bad when she heard that he might not be able to talk after the first burn injury. Getting rid of Athi was the only way out for her. She said that if we had offered to take him away from her, she would have agreed. She also agreed with me that if we had managed to ask her the right kind of questions, she might have come out with her real feelings.

She said that during her stay in the hospital she was feeling bad and depressed, she felt sorry for Athi, she also did not want him because of her fear of her husband. She did eat and sleep and she said she never heard voices or felt outside herself. Even when she went out for the weekends, she was always aware of what was hanging over her. She was interested to know how Athi was, she had been thinking about which language he would be talking. She very much wanted a photograph of him.

During her time in prison Nosakhele was learning to read and write, and could for the first time write to her mother. She writes in Xhosa but could understand what I was saying in English. The language spoken in the prison is mainly Afrikaans.

Epilogue

Athi adapted well in the children's home but was a sad little boy—self-contained, quiet, and generally developing adequately, but it was clear that something was amiss. He seemed desperate for an attachment figure, and it was unfortunate that he was in a children's home on such a long-term basis. He learnt to speak fluent Afrikaans. The one constant figure from his past was the head nurse of the ward—

she continued to have him with her and her family over weekends, and although she did not foster him, she never abandoned him.

When he was nine years old I saw him again, and it emerged that Athi had been to visit his mother in prison on three occasions and that active attempts were being made to locate his biological family. Nosakhele's sister was prepared to take him and make him "one of her own." She has two older boys and two younger sons, who were apparently waiting for "their brother" to come. At the time of the interview there was not much of a relationship between Athi and his aunt, and they could not communicate, as he could not speak isiXhosa. However, Athi was desperate to be with his family, and it was thus decided to introduce him slowly into rural life in the Eastern Cape. This was done, again with the help of the social worker and the head nurse, and from reports received to date he is happily integrated. He is due to have reconstructive maxillo-facial surgery soon. His mother has completed her term of imprisonment and has been released; she may well also be with him by this stage.

Athi clearly has a robust constitution; despite the trauma and deprivations of his early infancy, the disrupted attachment with his mother, and the multiple attachments that a children's home brings with it, he has managed to adapt to every situation. He has moved not only geographically but culturally and language wise from an urban, Afrikaans-English context to a rural indigenous and probably materially poor setting. By all accounts thus far received, he has adjusted. He is reported to have a gift for languages and speaks all three—English, Afrikaans, and isiXhosa—with ease.

His ability to bounce back, to make the best of what he has been offered, together with his mother's openness toward us, her honest description of her life and her deeds, is remarkable—they are testimonies to a resilience that is deeply rooted and speaks to a connection in terms of family and possibly spirituality that is protective and holding.

What Has Been Learned?

We did not grasp the true nature of Nosakhele's dilemma. We interpreted her nonbonding with Athi in a very simplistic manner—as though it would suffice if we were to teach her about the importance of attachment. This attitude came from a position of not understanding, but it also came from a wish to give mother and baby the best possible options available—the best being what western medicine and psychodynamic thinking had to offer. This tragedy took place during the early stages of the new South Africa, when many people were attempting to make up for the past by providing all people with equal access to good services and giving all equal opportunities.

It may well be that unconsciously, the fear was that by going too much into Nosakhele's difficult position, a sense of otherness would be discovered—and to focus on this otherness might be tantamount to wanting to categorize people because of their race group, something that had been so abhorrent to many. Leslie Swartz argues in a thought-provoking paper (Swartz 1996) that part of the struggle against the Apartheid regime involved de-emphasizing difference—everybody was the same; Apartheid had built itself on accentuating the otherness of the black people of the country. Culture thus was not an ideologically neutral concept. Talking about dissimilarity was practically the same as putting people down. It was only with the advent of democracy that differences between people could be affirmed and that diversity could be celebrated.

It must be emphasized that none of this was conscious—but there was a dynamic in the hospital ward and in the press that was powerful, and it arose out of the larger sociopolitical context in which the peoples of South Africa found themselves during those tumultuous times. No more were we going to repeat the past; now everyone was equal and many were thrilled by this. We were rescuing this baby, helping this mother, with all the best means available, with devotion and attention, but the effort failed.

The irony was that by making Nosakhele the same and giving her exactly the same treatment as we would have given a white mother, we missed the cultural dilemmas she was facing. We tried, perhaps too hard, to make her into a "good" mother, not wanting to look at the fact that she actually wanted to kill her baby, not wanting to make her a bad black mother. We were all so delighted, so encouraged by her positive interactions with her baby that we failed to see the nuances, the profound layers of her struggle. Her fall from grace came when the discovery of the poisoning was made; it was a dramatic fall. The move was from a position of wholeness to one of a split into the opposites. She immediately turned from the good mother into the terrible mother; even the court did not want to hear testimony that would have explained her actions. There was no redemption, and she received an unnecessarily harsh sentence, while Athi became the "divine" child, the one reported on by the press, the one many wanted to adopt.

We did not ask Nosakhele whether she actually wanted to keep her baby—it did not fit into the picture we were constructing of her. Not asking her this crucial question is something I have regretted deeply. The idealization of the good black mother and the vilification that ensued after the terrible deed attest to the fact that we were struggling with deep collective cultural complexes: we wished not to be racist, not to be prejudiced, but in that denial of difference we achieved the opposite—we left a young woman in an intolerable situation, one in which she and her infant were nonpersons, cut off from the very fabric that would have enveloped and held them.

But it is also through this not knowing that an urge arose to learn about the culture of my patients, because I had now learned through experience that it could be a matter of life and death if I did not. I have also come to know that only by inquiring about and acknowledging dissimilarity is one truly respectful of the other person.

How would I have handled a similar situation today? I would be far more rigorous in my inquiry as to which cultural traditions the family followed, and specifically I would ask what the meaning of the name was and why that name was chosen—much can be deduced from this. And I would not shy away from the question of whether the parents, the mother, wanted the baby or preferred that the child be cared for by another person or family. Having had the experience of what not-asking can result in, I feel quite sure within myself that issues have to be addressed—it is the place within oneself from whence these questions come that is the important part. If there is respect and caring, then even deep and very painful matters can be put into words.

CHAPTER 4

Ancestor Reverence

Athi and his tragic story were the motivation to understand another, non-European worldview more fully. The realization of the error came when the meaning of Athi's name was appreciated: "we thank the ancestors." How and where were the ancestors situated in the psyche of Nosakhele and millions of others? South Africa provides an unequaled opportunity for meeting: while on one level the dominant culture in urban parts of the country is of an industrialized, capitalist nature, in the rural areas and in those who have strong ties to their families there, traditions are observed in terms of indigenous rituals and ways of living. These groups form the majority in the country. There are thus many opportunities to engage with and ask about people's view of the world—there is an openness and willingness to share, as will be seen, as long as the request is a sincere one, and as long as it comes from a respectful place. At the same time no claim is made that all people from smaller towns and villages and cities subscribe to traditional African Religion (Mndende 2006)—many have long ago taken on Christianity as their way of being and living, and care needs to be taken not to make generalizing assumptions.

I owe much to my mentor and supervisor Vera Bührmann, who not only laid the foundation of the fundamentals of transcultural work but also provided us with a role model. The ability to be respectful and open is vital, while at the same time maintaining separateness and having a strong sense of identity, of where one comes from and who one is.

Although there is diversity among African cultures, commonalities are to be found in value systems and beliefs (Mnyaka 2003). Dr. Nokuzola Mndende, respected for her deep knowledge of African traditions, classifies the belief system under the term *African Religion* (Mndende 2006) and has observed: "Religion among Africans is not treated as an isolated entity: it is dealt with in a broader context since it permeates all sections of life of both the individual and the society" (ANC Commission 2006). This all-pervasiveness may be the reason Bührmann spoke of a "cosmology" rather than a religion. Moreover, through the years many people have converted to Christianity while still retaining reverence for their ancestors—indeed many churches actively combine the African way of being and believing with the Christian way. Christianity is then regarded more as "the religion." However, a traditionalist and academic like Mndende regards practicing both as incompatible and maintains that ancestor reverence and the rituals associated with it belong to African Religion and that one cannot simultaneously revere the ancestors and be a Christian (pers. comm., 2006).

Within the African worldview, or religion, are two axes that intersect (Berg 2003b). The vertical one encompasses ancestor reverence while the horizontal line belongs to *ubuntu* (described in detail in chapter 6). These two lines interweave and form the weft and warp of a cloth that contains and holds the psyche on a fundamental plane—it can be said to form the content of the cultural unconscious. Understanding these two axes and how they determine thinking and behavior is crucial to truly being respectful. Ancestor reverence could be said to pertain to the ego-self axis as described by Edinger, "the gateway or path of communication between the conscious personality and the objective psyche" (Edinger 1960, 9), or the spiritual axis. *Ubuntu* could be seen to belong to what could be called the ego-other

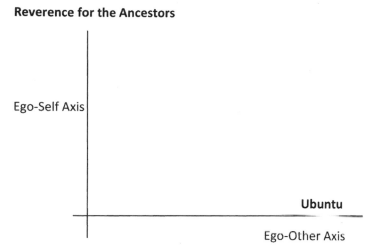

Reverence for the Ancestors

Ego-Self Axis

Ubuntu

Ego-Other Axis

The two intersecting axes within African religion are the spiritual dimension of ancestor reverence and the community-oriented dimension of ubuntu.

axis—the community dimension. At the many points of intersection they intertwine, and one cannot be without the other. However, for purposes of explanation, they are described separately.

Bührmann emphasizes the challenges that face a researcher when there are cultural differences and stresses the importance of having an attitude as free as possible of preconceived theories and prejudices. During her field trips she became a participant observer (Bührmann 1978). She spent days observing the healer, his wife, and their trainees in different situations and then recorded what she heard and saw. This way of working is closely aligned to the method of infant observation developed by Harris and Bick (Harris and Bick 1976). The task is to find the right position, the right distance, so as to experience and feel but still have mental space for observing what is happening outside and inside oneself. Bührmann managed to find this position under taxing circumstances. Having had the privilege of her supervision and teaching over many years, I was sensitized to this approach.

The awareness of attempting to have no prejudices, of having an open mind, of truly listening to and observing the other person, has been a treasured gift that I received from her.

And so it came to be that I had an opportunity to put myself in that position—albeit much diluted, as I was spared a long journey and a lengthy stay away from home. The ceremony I was able to attend occurred in an urban setting. Following is a description of the sequence of events and how I experienced them, after which I step back and give a more objective view of the structure of the ceremony and the meaning of some of the details.

A Personal Experience of Ancestor Reverence

Participation in a ritual of honoring the ancestors was made possible through my co-worker Nosisana Nama. My experience was a small part of a ceremony that had been performed over an entire weekend. What was striking was the similarity of this urban ritual and what Bührmann had described in her studies in the rural community.

Nosisana's aunt on her husband's side was in the final stages of becoming a traditional healer. However, "things were not going right for her," and she required an *intlombe,* which is a ritual performed indoors. This was not a major ritual, as no slaughtering of an animal was required, only the brewing of *umqombothi,* which is traditional beer.

The brewing in itself is a ritual: it is an almost week-long process during which certain taboos are observed—the woman is not allowed to wear modern clothes, such as jeans, but has to wear a dress and headscarf; she abstains from sexual encounters, and the beer is brewed in a very particular way, some even using particular containers. All this occurs before the weekend of the actual ceremony, which usually starts on a Friday.

Nosisana and I arrived at the house late on a Sunday morning. It was a hot midday, and the open spaces were dusty. Outside a group of children played. Nosisana asked me to park the car where it would be visible from the house, as there were "naughty boys" around—a sign of the criminal element so inevitable in our rapidly changing society, particularly in the urban areas. I waited for a short while outside while Nosisana went into the house, which was built of brick and painted blue-green. We entered the small living room where there were chairs and benches along three walls. About fifteen people were already sitting there. A chair was made available for me immediately, and I felt that I was being treated as a special visitor. Nosisana positioned herself opposite me on a bench, between two elderly men.

In the center of the room stood six aluminum cans of *umqombothi*, together with seven bottles of soft drinks, cans of Gold and Hunter's beer, and a bottle of brandy. A plate with some coins in it also stood there with a tray of empty glasses. The mix of western and African culture was manifest in this central place. Nosisana instructed me to place in the center the vodka bottle she had advised me to bring. I was thanked profusely, and one old woman kissed my hand, which I reciprocated. We then sat for quite some time while people were waiting and talking. Most persons present were older people, but there were also two younger men. I was struck by the many children walking in an out, unperturbed by the events in the living room; it was clear that they considered this in quite an ordinary way—this is what happens from time to time in their homes, and there is nothing special about it. This is indeed how culture is transmitted from one generation to the next.

The leader of the events, the healer or *iqhirha*, was an impressive woman behind the drums. She sat diagonally opposite the door on a chair in the corner. She had an ordinary dress on, bright pink, with an imposing green scarf on her head. She was barefooted. To her right side three women dressed in white were sitting on the floor. One was Nosisana's aunt, about sixty years old, dressed in a white skirt and blouse with black lines sewn onto the white. This is the traditional festive Xhosa outfit, and the white depicts that the person is the initiate. On her forehead with wispy hair, she wore white beads, and she had a white and black bag over one shoulder. Behind the three women a large goat skin decorated the wall.

An older man who seemed to be the second in charge of the ceremony and who sat opposite the healer took a can of the traditional beer and kneeled down in front of me and drank some. He then offered me the can, and I was told to kneel down in order to drink of it. He repeated this with the other participants. Later the brandy and vodka were offered to all in a small glass, but one did not have to kneel down for receiving this. One trainee healer threw a few drops on the carpet—this was meant for the ancestors.

Nosisana's aunt for whom the ceremony was organized lit a pipe, put her false teeth in her bag, and hung it onto the goat skin. The healer started drumming and singing, and the aunt started dancing. The power of the drumming and singing was immense. Soon she was joined by the other two trainees, who had sticks in their hands, and all of us were clapping in synchrony with the dancing and drumming. The dancing of the three women was remarkable in the forceful thumping of their bare feet, with the rhythm visibly reverberating in their whole bodies. At times the dancing would be stopped and the healer would speak to the aunt. The rest of the people would reply *camagu*, which means "we agree." What the healer said sounded at times forceful and angry—accompanied by an outward thrusting movement of her arms and hands. She often had to wipe her face from perspiration. I was told later that the aunt had been asked to tell a dream, which she could not. She was asked whether the presence of a white person was the problem, but she replied no, as her ancestors had accepted me.

After a while the young woman from the house was called. She was made to kneel down in front of the trainees. They spoke, and later the healer spoke. She was told that there was trouble in her home and that she needed to sort things out with her parents-in-law. The young woman listened in silence and, when the talk was completed, went to the back of her house again, smiling. The rest of her household had through all this time continued in the kitchen, with young children walking to and fro—none were unnerved by the happenings in the living room.

I was then told to go back to my chair (as I had been standing in one corner) and was told by the healer that my health was good but that I had worries. She said I wanted to bring black and white people together—I wanted to do this for the world. Then she said that there was something else worrying me, but that she would rather tell me this in private. I felt quite stunned by the accuracy of what she had said and rather apprehensive of meeting her in private, as indeed, at the time I did have another worry.

An older man in the audience was then told that he was not living according to his ancestors, but like a Coloured (that is, not like a black African), and that he needed to go on the path of healing. He listened respectfully and smiled. At the end of this part of the ceremony the healer and Nosisana's aunt came outside with us to greet us farewell. On our asking her whether she was tired, the healer said, "No, I am not working today."

Returning to my home in middle-class, western surroundings, I was initially disoriented. I had been through an amazing and awesome experience, and it was only a few kilometers away from the city center. I realized how far away culturally we were from each other—black and white—how we had no idea of what was being enacted, who was being revered by the majority of our fellow citizens.

African Religion

I would now like to reflect on some aspects of this small part of the ritual of honoring and connecting with the ancestors in which I was a participant. By way of definition, a ceremony is a formal act or set of acts performed as prescribed by ritual or custom; a ritual is a formalized, predetermined set of symbolic actions.

The ritual is thus the overarching event, such as the ritual of marriage, whereas the ceremony is that which comprises the symbolic enactment related to that event, such as the wedding ceremony itself. In African indigenous cultures there exists an interaction with the supernatural world; there is no passive contemplation but an active engagement through various acts. "We here enter the realm of ritual, both religious and magical, the techniques man has devised to manage satisfactorily his relations with gods, nature and other men. Ritual forms the articulation point between the belief system and the network of day-to-day interactions between men which is society. It is here that the social and ideational interpenetrate" (Hammond-Tooke 1937, 344).

The sharing of the traditional beer with the ancestors by pouring it onto the ground (the carpet, in this case) is one of those points where the social and ideational interpenetrate, where there is magic. Similarly, the manner in which the young woman was called in and told that things in her home were not as they should be, and the apparent calm way in which she received this news, meant that a higher injunction was being followed or obeyed. But what about the ceremony that surrounded these magical moments? Before looking in more detail at the structure of that afternoon, an explanation needs to be given to situate those happenings within the greater cosmology of this African belief system.

The healer, academic, and cultural consultant Nokuzola Mndende cites three basic beliefs that pertain to African Religion:

1. Belief in the Creator, the Spirit, who is neither male nor female. Creation began in the spiritual world "which is regarded as holy, and where the laws, rituals and taboos that control the welfare of the physical world originated" (Mndende 2006, 3).

2. Belief in the ancestors—those who have passed away from the physical world to the spiritual world. Death is understood as a partial physical separation from the living, and hence the dead are "asleep" and have not wholly disappeared. While people come and go, relationships within the clan do not end. The ancestors act as guides and protectors for the living and they provide intercession to the higher power of the spirit. The sense of protection the ancestors offer the living is profound and can supersede western education and Christian doctrine.

3. The practice of rituals (amasiko; Mndende 2006, 3). These rituals have to do with life events, such as marriage and burial, but are also individually determined, to give thanks or such as when a dream indicates that something is amiss. No general predetermined calendar of events and festivals exists: the need for a ritual comes from within the individual or family. Similarly, there are no general physical structures where these ceremonies are conducted, such as a church, synagogue, or mosque. They happen in the home or homestead where the family lives

and where the ancestors also reside. The ceremonies that form part of the ritual of ancestor reverence are called *intlombe*. The ritual serves to maintain or restore the link with the ancestors, to ensure their goodwill and guidance, and to protect people from the evils of witchcraft. Rituals may also help to establish the *why* and *who* of events (Bührmann 1984). What Bührmann described in rural, natural surroundings remains essentially unchanged in an urban, more industrialized environment.

There are two types of rituals: those that are deeply embedded and part of the cultural psyche, and that are unlikely to change, are named *isiko*. Those that have more to do with customs and that could change over time are called *isithethe*. The rituals described here belong to the first group.

Four aspects of this *intlombe* require further analysis if we are to understand more fully the healing function of this kind of ritual (Berg 2003b). The concepts of containment and linking, as described and elaborated by W. R. Bion (1962), are helpful in understanding why ceremonies like these have a positive effect on the whole person.

The Physical Mandala

Bührmann (1981) described the four-ringed structure of this indoor ritual in great detail. The outer ring consists of the walls of the hut,

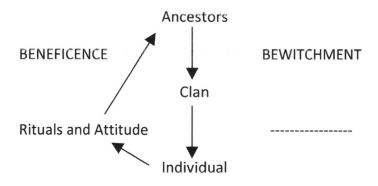

The cycle of exposure of individuals and their protection by ancestors.

or in our case the walls of the house, followed by the circle formed by the family and community—this was where we sat; and then the circle formed by the dancers. The fourth is the very center—where the hearth is—the place of warmth and food. Bührmann observes that these circles essentially embody the structure of the universal mandala—the word itself actually meaning "circle" in Sanskrit. If we accept Jung's interpretation that the concentric circles of the mandala "shut out the outside and hold the inside together" (Jung 1977, 356), then we can see how these two human and two nonhuman circles of the *intlombe* form a container or *temenos* within which encounters can occur: encounters on a vertical plane—with the ancestors, and encounters on a horizontal plane—with the community. The training healer was in turmoil, as was the young woman who lived in the house, as was the man who was told off for not honoring the ancestors: these three people's difficulties were not necessarily solved, but they were acknowledged and heard by all who were present.

Involvement of the Community

Consultations with traditional healers are seldom done alone—they are matters that affect the family and are determined by the family, usually the elders. A direct referral to a traditional healer cannot be made by an outsider, someone who is representing western medicine. That decision is left for the family and, as a western-trained doctor, one can only stand back and allow the process to unfold. Z. C. Nqweni (1999) compares the *intlombe* with western group psychotherapy, and much of what she argues was evident in the session described here.

The healer is the clearly defined "conductor" of the therapeutic process and is more than the facilitator and fellow participant we see with the usual western therapeutic group. The responses during the *intlombe* are directed to all those present, on behalf of the patient; this was seen when the trainee healer could not give an account of her dream—other people in the room were being addressed. Because the healer is acting on behalf of the ancestors, she had the authority to be direct and directive in her approach—the guidance comes

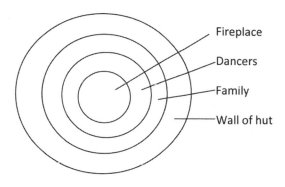

Fireplace

Dancers

Family

Wall of hut

The four-ringed physical mandala of the intlombe ritual.

from the unconscious, in western terms, and not from the ego of the healer. This is very different to a western group therapy setting, where there is free-floating discussion and where each group member takes responsibility for his or her actions and words. It is then also mainly through the verbal modality that catharsis is achieved, whereas in a traditional ceremony this occurs through drumming, singing, clapping, and movement.

Involvement of the Body

Bührmann suggests that the *intlombe* is "a mandala in action" (Bührmann 1981, 188), and it is the circle of clapping and dancing participants around the very center that forms the crux of this mandala in action. The healer was the drummer in our session, and that formed the background rhythm to the clapping and singing of the community; the patient and two other trainee healers were the main participants, and they proceeded to dance by circumambulating the center. This dance is a particular one, and is called a *xhentsa*—it is an expressive movement that consists of pounding bare feet into the ground while slowly moving in a circle, while the upper part of the body is kept fairly still except for the clapping of the hands and singing of special songs. The *xhentsa* is regarded as a way to express feelings (Bührmann 1981, 188). While the actual dancing was limited to particular persons, all who were in the room were singing and clapping. This created a sense of togetherness and harmony but also of participation with what was happening to the patient—aiding and encouraging her with her process.

Dreams

The telling of the dream was a highlight of the session, or should have been, but in this case its recall seemed to have been blocked, and a reason had to be found for this. "The dream is to see the truth at night . . . the dreams are the truth because the ancestors never deceive their children" (Bührmann 1984, 50); in its simplicity this quotation from Bührmann's book contains so much. Without dreams the healer cannot work. Dreams are one of the main ways in which the ancestors communicate with the living; dreams form part of daily living, and are talked about, and their meaning needs to be found. In a traditional family they may be taken to the elders, who will confer and think about a dream and decide on the appropriate actions. Dreams are part of the family and community life—they do not belong in a therapist's office, and they are not routinely brought to a healer. Only once the family decides that a dream requires this type of intervention is a healer consulted. The interpretation of a dream is also often more literal—that is, leading to an outside action. Despite some differences in dream interpretation, Bührmann found that her understanding had much in common with that of the healer whom she consulted (Bührmann 1978). From a western perspective, what differs more is the general acceptance of the importance of dreams, the ordinary way in which they are discussed, and the involvement of the family and community in the dreams of the individual, as was seen in the small part of the ceremony described.

Making Links

As human beings we require meaning to be made of what happens to us. Making links between thoughts, between inner and outer happenings, forms the backbone of any psychoanalytically informed clinical practice. Understanding these connections is what brings relief to psychic pain and conflict. While this psychological relief often also has an effect on the person's physical well-being, the focus, generally speaking, is not on the body. A different therapeutic modality has to be sought in order for that to occur. Similarly, the family and the community in which the patient lives are talked about but are not literally brought into the session, again unless the approach sought out is specifically a family therapy approach.

The *intlombe* combines these various parts into one whole therapeutic experience. A western-oriented therapist might be troubled at the intensity, length, and multi-modality of these sessions. In classical psychoanalytic terms, the apparent transgression of boundaries might seem alarming, as this could lead to a lowering of consciousness, weakening of ego defenses, and consequent "acting out" by those involved in the ceremony. However, this anxiety is not evident in the healer or the participants.

What enables this space to be used in what appears to be such a constructive way? It must be noted that the majority of the black African population of South Africa consult with traditional as well as western-oriented health professionals (Campbell-Hall et al. 2010). Traditional healers are viewed as being able to determine the cause of illness, and if this is attributed to a gap in the relationship with the ancestors, healing rituals are performed. Despite urbanization and sociopolitical changes, these traditions remain alive. The therapeutic benefits that such rituals have appear to be profound.

The containment offered by the mandala-like physical structure provides a safe physical space in which thoughts and feelings can be expressed. But there is more to it than merely an outer configuration of holding. As Nqweni has suggested, the healer becomes the voice of the ancestors or the conduit for their voices—this is what gives her the power and ultimately her confidence and surety.

This is echoed in Levi-Strauss's (1963) description of the shaman. He analyzes a particular text from South America, a song intended to facilitate a difficult childbirth seen to be caused by the spirits, who have made the mother lose her soul. The shaman intervenes through incantation and in this way battles for the return of her conquered soul. Levi-Strauss writes:

But the shaman does more than utter the incantation; he is its hero, for it is he who, at the head of a supernatural battalion of spirits, penetrates the endangered organs and frees the captive soul. In this way he, like the psychoanalyst, becomes the object of transference and, through the representations induced in the patient's mind, the real protagonist of the conflict which the latter experiences on the border between the physical and the psychic world. (Levi-Strauss 1963, 199)

Here too it can be seen that the healer in an indigenous ceremony becomes more than an individual man or woman—having transcended the boundaries into the beyond and become the mediator between those on the other side and those on this side. This inner certainty affects the way in which the healer takes charge of the ceremony and the way in which the participants engage with the process. The "centeredness" thus comes more from within the psyche than from without.

As It Was Yesterday, So It Is Today

Although what I observed and participated in was a small part of a much longer ceremony, it did convey the power of the ritual of making contact with and honoring the ancestors. What was particularly striking was the fact that all of this, as described by Vera Bührmann from a rural area years before, was actually happening in the city and in this modern day and age. What was shameful was the fact that as a white South African I had no idea of this happening in my neighborhood, so to speak. For a few hours that Sunday morning, I was participating in a world that was foreign to me, but it is a world many of my patients inhabit. Had I known more about its power and its influence on personhood, the psychotherapy with Athi's mother might have gone along a completely different path. The following chapter illustrates the extent of this influence on personhood even more clearly.

CHAPTER 5

An Adolescent Rite of Passage

WHAT CAN WE LEARN FROM AFRICAN CULTURE?

Talking about culture and taking pride in our multicultural society have become possible only since the dismantling of Apartheid. Colonial rule from the very beginning sought to reinforce notions of cultural and racial distinction in order to justify legislation that played on difference and thereby tried to provide legitimacy for the "separate development." Understandably, in politicized academic circles it was simply not done to focus on any aspect that spoke to dissimilarity, and many thus eschewed talking about culture. All too easily it could be regarded as collaborating with the repressive regime.

From personal communication I know that Vera Bührmann suffered a great deal from this attitude prevailing at a time when she was consulting at Valkenberg Hospital (the local mental hospital) during the 1980s. Her connection to and understanding of the patients' inner world was obvious, but the discomfort felt when she spoke about cultural issues on a more academic level was such that she eventually stopped doing these psychiatric consultations. Thankfully in the new South Africa talk about culture in the general population is welcomed. Our professional black African colleagues, however, have until fairly recently felt reluctant to voice opinions about or display their knowledge of traditional culture. This possibly had to do with a fear of being judged by their westernized superiors, but the syndrome is gradually fading.

To talk and write about cultural traditions that are not one's own is a challenge; but there may also be an advantage—standing on the outside often gives one a perspective that is less apparent to those on the inside. A culture that is alive and has meaning should be treasured and should be documented, as much can be learned from it. This not only holds for South Africans living in a diverse society; it also applies globally. The world consists of many different cultural groupings, and clashes may occur unless an effort is made from all sides, particularly by those who feel themselves to be superior, to understand and meet with the other.

What is shared in this chapter is an attempt at that. It pertains to a particular phase of life—childhood and its transition to adulthood—and it belongs to a particular cultural group; but the principles involved in trying to understand these rites of passage could serve as an example of engagement and dialogue. A word of caution is necessary at this point, because what is described belongs to a deep cultural tradition that has taboos attached to it. The adolescent rite of passage belongs to the male world, a world of which women should not have intimate knowledge. In addition to a non-Xhosa woman attempting to elucidate this process, there is also the desire to underpin it with psychology—and "white man's psychology," at that. I acknowledge the delicateness of this situation and hope that what is revealed is presented with respect and will be held with respect.

Last, and perhaps most important, much of what I relate is no longer as it was meant to be. Although there has been no decline in the wish to be circumcised—some ten thousand Xhosa men are circumcised annually in the Eastern Cape (Vincent 2008)—there has been a decay in the strict rules that used to govern this process. What used to be a carefully planned and executed ritual has given way to money making and profiteering by untrained persons who practice as traditional surgeons and nurses. This leads to unnecessary deaths of young men and unacceptable medical complications (Kepe 2010). These are tragic and in no way to be condoned or denied. One of the underlying reasons for this decay and its devastating consequences is the breakup of family life and family obligations. Thando Mgqolozana's recent *A Man Who Is Not a Man* (Mgqolozana 2009) is a brave description of his failed circumcision, the young man's anger at the older men in his family for having let him down, and how he has found his way to true manhood. He does not dismiss the practice, but he is justifiably critical of its neglect in terms of male responsibility.

The motivation to take the risks of writing about this is the wish to bring a psychological perspective to a topic that ethnographers and anthropologists have researched but that has not received much attention from the psychoanalytic world. The wish is to show that we can learn from indigenous cultures. I do not mean to come across as prescriptive, nor do I presume to know all about circumcision; and in particular I am not saying that this is what should happen to all Xhosa-speaking males. The European psyche can be particularly susceptible to fascination with African culture—it is a need for compensation and, for white South Africans, it may have to do with guilt. I am aware of the guilt component, but the greater driver for me is the fact that in my clinical capacity I have to know about the customs of my patients. I do feel ashamed of not having known more before, and I stand amazed at the richness of the traditions of my fellow South Africans; however, I am also acutely aware of the danger of romantically idealizing indigenous culture. Mamphela Ramphele correctly regards this as a form of racism (Ramphele 2008).

As Athi, who has taught me so much, is a boy, and as the adolescent rite of passage described here concerns boys and men only, this chapter is concerned with the emotional and social development of the boy child. A description of the closeness of the mother-son bond is followed by a description of a childhood ritual that has to precede the ritual of adolescence into adulthood.

In the Beginning

Universally it could be said that the conception of a child is predated by fantasies about a child and about motherhood. The infant thus starts off as an internal object in the mother's mind. However, after conception, at about sixteen weeks gestation, the fetus makes its separateness felt through its first movements—that first kick could be regarded as the first act of individuality noted by the mother. Modern infant research has shown that the baby is aware of its separateness from the very beginning (Stern 1985). However, this separateness is relative: the infant is completely dependent on the mother, and without a primary relationship psychic and physical death can ensue. We are reminded of Rene Spitz's institutionalized babies of the 1940s; observing them prompted him to coin the term *anaclitic depression*. They had all the physical care they required but still presented with deeply disturbed behavior (Spitz 1946). The close relationship between mother and child is thus necessary not only for physical growth but also for psychological development. Without fantasies being woven around the child, there is nothing for the child to grow into.

This early physical dependence is followed by a lengthy process whereby children work out and work through their emotional ties to parents. Sigmund Freud posited the notion that the emotional tie to the self and to the parent is of the same type of energy out of which later adult sexual relationships develop (Freud 1974). He simply called it the sexuality or libidinal drive of the infant, while Jung preferred the wider term *eros*. Whatever term we use, the point is that the tie to the primary love objects is strong and needs to be resolved for the sake of the future of the human race. The triangular relationship between child, mother, and father and its resolution was placed at the center of Freudian theory. Jung did challenge whether this was the only universal complex, but he accepted it as a primary one.

The Oedipal situation is one whereby the boy, being in love with his mother and wishing to marry her, realizes that he cannot do so, as the mother belongs to the father; in fantasy he fears the father's revenge on him should he dare take the mother away. He thus defends against this wish of marrying his mother by identifying with his father and later on choosing another sexual partner. This is the resolution of the Oedipus complex.

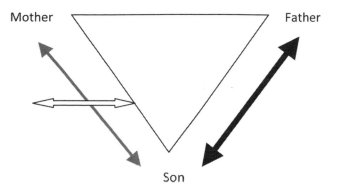

Jung accepted the Oedipal triangle relationship of mother, father, and son.

This double separation that the young male child has to make from his mother—separation from physical dependence and then from his love for her—is a huge psychological task. Indeed the resolution of the Oedipal conflict is a heroic struggle, and it is this struggle that is at the heart of many a fairy tale and myth. The pull back to the mother is a strong one, which we all have. But particularly for the growing boy it is a constant battle not to succumb; equally, for the mother it means resisting her urges to envelop her son with her love, and she can only hope to have a son who draws the line in the sand.

In my work with mothers and infants and toddlers, one of the most frequent presenting complaints coming from westernized mothers is that of separation anxiety—either their own, as regards leaving their child, or the child's, as regards being separated from his mother. It manifests itself most frequently in the very young child in sleep disturbances. Conflicts about whether it is permissible to sleep with one's baby and whether one should pick babies up whenever they cry cause much anxiety in mothers. They consult books, they consult professionals. Many do not have the confidence to do what they feel is right for them and the baby—they have to hear it from somebody else. They also have the sense that all depends on them—that if they make a mistake, it will be devastating to the child. There is no recourse to the helping hands of others.

This contrasts quite starkly with the mothers seen in the community clinic in Khayelitsha. The great majority of these mothers come from the Eastern Cape, where their families of origin reside. This means that culturally speaking, most of them are connected to those rituals and ceremonies belonging to the amaXhosa. The presenting complaint in coming to our clinic has never been sleep disturbance in the young infant, nor have there been questions around sleeping arrangements. Partly this is because there is not much choice for alternative sleeping measures, but it is also that there is not the same kind of anxiety about separation between mother and child. The child is carried on the mother's back for much of the time and is breastfed completely on demand, without counting of feeds. The infant sleeps with the mother until such time as he chooses to sleep elsewhere—this natural separation occurs usually during toddlerhood.

Why is there this stark difference? Why is the anxiety around separation so prevalent with western mothers and so absent with the African mothers I know? My hypothesis is that perhaps African mothers are able to give themselves over to the primal union with a child without anxiety, as they know, consciously or unconsciously, that when the time is right, their sons will be separated from them and that thereby the incest taboo will be respected. Even in the absence of the biological father, a mother can be assured that a male member of the father's clan (or a male member of the mother's clan, if the father has been completely nonexistent for the child) will be involved in the adolescent rite of passage, thereby making sure that the link to the masculine is strengthened. Mothers are rarely alone in their child rearing. Of course this is shifting rapidly in urbanized areas, and such generalizations could be seen as naïve and simplistic. However, despite this, it is a clinical observation that has been made over many years and with many mother-infant dyads—this may not be the only reason for the seeming lack of separation neurosis, but culture could well be a protective factor against anxiety.

Before describing two rituals that are performed regularly by the vast majority of the Xhosa people with whom I have come into contact, I want to set the stage by showing how ancestor reverence is conveyed from very early on in life.

Reverence for the Ancestors Starts in the Cradle

The ancestors are the "living dead," members of the family and clan who have died but continue to live as "shades." There is a human, alive relationship between the individual and his or her ancestors—they act as guides and mentors. They manifest themselves through dreams and bodily sensations. The relationship is a symbiotic one (Bührmann 1984), with the living keeping the deceased in mind and honoring them through ceremonies, in return for receiving their protection. Only if the protection is withdrawn can bad things, such as bewitchment, occur.

One of the ways the child is already being attuned to his ancestors is through a traditional chant in which the mother praises her child by situating him in his clan. Following are translated extracts from such a praise song heard in Khayelitsha in August 1999:

> *Mommy's boy, Mommy's boy*
> *Loved by his mother [four times]*
> *Small boy loved by his mother*
> *Small boy loved by his mother*
> *His mother loves him*
> *He is Ayanda*
> *Ayanda Amagubevu*
> *Ayanda Amagubevu*
> *Ayanda Amagubevu*
> *The Magubevus are increasing*

In reciting and repeating clan names, showing the clan getting bigger, more numerous, and more important, this mother is placing her fourteen-week-old son in a long chain of clan ancestors—she is telling him where his place is and does this in a steady monotone, which comforts and settles him. At the formative stage of this little boy's core self (Stern 1985), he not only receives a sense of physical holding but also a sense of greater belonging. This is an example of how culture, the shared meaning of a group, provides the infant with a sense of identity right from the very beginning of life (Emde 2006).

Unlike Athi, who did not have this privilege, Ayanda has probably continued to grow well and may by now have had the experience of his first traditional ritual, namely that of being formally introduced to his ancestors. The praise song was an event, an experience that occurred between him and his mother; it was situated within the dyad and is probably part of his implicit memory. A more public, community-oriented ceremony is needed in order to share more explicitly the joy of his belonging to this family, this clan, and these ancestors.

This ceremony is called the *imbeleko* and is a prerequisite for the adolescent rite of passage, much as baptism precedes first communion or confirmation in the Christian church. It serves the function of a formal, public introduction of the child to his ancestors and their acceptance of him. It can be done at any point during childhood; much depends on whether the family has the money to fund this occasion. From the description that follows, it is clear why this is a costly affair.

Imbeleko—Introduction to the Ancestors

I had the great fortune and privilege to participate in parts of this ritual for the three children of my co-worker Nosisana Nama. The eldest, Thembela, a young woman now living in the Cape Town suburb called Nyanga and working as an accountant in Stellenbosch, later gave me this description:

> The family gathered together on Friday afternoon. The children had a nanny, a sister to the father, who has had an *mbeleko*. The children were introduced to their goats one by one and the three goats were slaughtered for each child. For girls it will be a female goat, and for boys a male goat. The man took the *isinga* [tendon] just next to the spine of each goat. This will be used to make the *intambo* or necklace with white beads that are used for rituals. *Umkhono* of each goat, the meat is called *umshwamo*, will be braaied [i.e., a shoulder is roasted] for each child inside the house on Friday and they can eat it afterwards.

The [other *umkhono*] will be cooked the following day for each child. No one is allowed to eat these parts unless one had undergone the same process before. The ritual must be done by a family member (man) of the same clan. A person who knows what he is doing. If this part goes wrong, it will create problems in the child's future.

On Saturday the whole goat will be cooked for family, friends and visitors. The children's entire bodies are smeared with ocre by a senior member of the father's clan. Before dining, each person present will be given two beads that will be used for the *intambo* to keep until they are taken back from them. (The beads are accepted with the left hand and given back with the right hand.) A person chosen by the family to do the *intambo* will do it after eating. When they are ready, each child will be given his or hers. They will be dressed by the elder who was conducting the ceremony.

On Sunday morning the nanny will wake up early to cook the leg which was left behind and each family member present in the house will eat from that leg before leaving the house. All the bones from Friday and Saturday will be kept in one place safely and burnt on the Sunday afternoon. The children will wear the *intambo* as a necklace until it breaks on its own and it will be collected and burnt at once. If the necklace is lost, the children must not look for it, and they are not to worry.

To look at some of these actions more closely: there is clear aligning of the children with their father's clan, which in fact excluded their mother's direct participation—she remained in the background, although all this took place in her home. The choice of the animal is important—either a goat or a cow is needed for ritual slaughtering, the reason being that both bleat on being stabbed with the special spear. A sheep is silent, and is thus not used. The significance of this bleating is that the ancestors approve—it means a direct connecting of those on the other side with those on this side.

It is a moment equivalent to the consecration in the Catholic Mass; that moment when Christ is present—as though a curtain of time and space is torn or opened. According to Jung, with the speaking of the words of the consecration a mystical unity occurs: "At this moment the eternal character of the one divine sacrifice is made evident: it is experienced at a particular time and a particular place, as if a window or a door had been opened upon that which lies beyond space and time" (Jung 1969a, 214).

In the indigenous African setting the bleating of the goat or cow is needed. The fact that the child's ancestors specifically accept the child makes this a more personal, more family-oriented ritual than that of Christian baptism, where uniform words and actions constitute the ritual.

The eating of this meat then represents the literal incorporation of the ancestors, taking them into oneself, making them part of oneself. Again there are equivalents to the celebration of the Holy Mass.

Using the tendon that comes from the spinal cord as a basis for the necklace means a joining of the individual with the ancestors, but there is an important additional element: the beads are white. White "is the colour that symbolizes a special relationship with the ancestral spirits" (Shaw 1937, 103). Across many cultures white symbolizes the sacred, the holy. For example, Osiris and the priests of Israel were clothed in white, and medieval paintings portray God in garments of white (Evarts 1919). These white beads have to be held by the family and community—first in the left hand, then given back with the right hand. In Jungian psychology the rational, conscious contents of the ego are associated with the left side, and the unconscious, more emotional part with the right hemisphere (Rossi 1977). Two processes could be said to take place with this one movement: the two sides, left and right, are integrated, and the beads move from the unconscious to consciousness. The Latin *particeps* means to "take part": the making of the intambo during the child's ancestral ritual has in it, very literally, a part of every person present.

Thembela's account says the children wear the intambo as a necklace "until it breaks on its own and it will be collected and burnt at once. If the necklace is lost, the children must not look for it, and they are not to worry." Does this perhaps place the intambo in the realm of the transitional object that Winnicott (1971) describes so eloquently?

Is it an object that belongs to the space between two worlds? For the infant the soft blanket occupies that space where it represents mother and yet not mother, where "inner and outer reality [are] separate yet interrelated" (3). The fate of the transitional object is to be dissolved—"it is not forgotten and it is not mourned. It loses meaning, and this is because the transitional phenomena have become diffused, have become spread out over the whole intermediate territory between 'inner psychic reality' and 'the external world as perceived by two persons in common,' that is to say, over the whole cultural field" (6).

The intambo stands for the connection with the ancestors and the connection with the community—it gets worn until it breaks, or it may get lost. If it breaks it has to be burned, because it cannot be reconstituted—like the baby blanket or teddy that gets washed and then loses its meaning for the child, so a broken intambo loses its power and its bits have to be obliterated. However, where it does remain is in the psyche of the individual and the community—in the transitional field or in the cultural conscious and unconscious of the child, the family, and the group.

This is but a small sample of what occurs during traditional rituals. Many more such concrete manifestations of participation exist on all these various levels. Unfortunately they go unrecorded, as they are simply there; that is how it is done and how it has been done since time immemorial, and there is not much to debate around it—it is up to each person to think about it, to process it internally. Words are not needed. In this there is a depth and sophistication of thinking that is not easily visible, that remains unarticulated, unless one has the privilege of engaging closely with an individual of that tradition.

Because the community at large attends, all will know that the *imbeleko* has been done for this child; there is no need for a certificate or proof. In addition each child has a mat from this time—and this mat is what the boy takes with him to the bush, for the next ritual.

Introduction to Manhood

Becoming a man is probably the most crucial moment in a boy's life, especially when it is marked by an actual event, one that has been planned for and is known about within the whole family and community. For the indigenous group to which Athi belongs and who live mainly in the Eastern and Western Cape, ritual male circumcision is practiced to mark the beginning of manhood. It is one of the most sacred rites (Vincent 2008) and is associated with many taboos; obtaining information about it is difficult.

Circumcision is probably the oldest known planned surgical procedure (Alanis and Lucidi 2004), having been practiced by the Egyptians even before reference is made to it in the Old Testament. The first report of Xhosa circumcision dates to 1686, when survivors of the Dutch East India Company's ship the *Stavenisse* observed the coming out ceremony of a young man. A century later more reports were received from travelers to the area, and the first full-scale monograph was written in 1805 (Ngxamngxa 1971). The tradition has remained alive in its essence in many groups in South Africa. For example, research carried out in 2003 for the multimedia program *Soul Buddyz*, which addresses contemporary issues around gender and masculinity, asked young people between the ages of eight and fourteen: "What do boys do that makes them boys?" The answer invariably was: "It is going to initiation (*ukoluka*)" (Clachterty and Associates 2003, 11). The boys who came from the Eastern Cape regarded becoming a man as occurring only after having gone to initiation school.

There are many variations of this rite of passage, but in broad outline, similar patterns are followed in different regions; circumcision is commonly part of the process, though this is not invariably so in all groups (van der Vliet 1974). What follows is a description that is limited to the amaXhosa, who are the main black African group living in and around Cape Town. The information was obtained not only through literature but from patient material as well as from informal conversations with colleagues and ordinary people. The themes that emerged from these contacts were consistent, and there appeared to be no contradictions or disputed issues. Much was also verified in Thando Mgqolozana's autobiographical account, already mentioned. The background provided by analytical psychology was helpful in grasping themes and in asking the right kind of questions. The role Vera Bührmann played in laying the ground for this further inquiry is deeply acknowledged (Berg 2007).

The abakwetha (the initiates) of male circumcision are showcased in paintings by
A. H. Barrett for 1979 postage stamps issued by the amaXhosa "homeland"
of Transkei. Rituals include body painting, dancing, and burning a
specially constructed hut in symbolic farewell to childhood.

The Ukoluka Ritual

The *ukoluka* is carried out when the boy is ready to assume the re-sponsibility of a man; that is, toward the end of adolescence, when he is about to complete his schooling and enter the adult world of work-ing and of marriage. However, as with the *imbeleko*, considerable cost is involved, and the family has to be able to afford sending their son to this initiation school. These schools are activated during the longer summer and winter school vacations. In modern times part of the preparations for going into the "bush" (as it is colloquially known) consists of a medical examination and antibiotic cover, and often a sterile blade is provided.

This is followed by a farewell from home. For some a big send-off from the homestead is organized, with songs being invented and shared—the hopes of the mother and community being expressed in these. In the case of Thando Mgqolozana an all-night vigil was held (Mgqolozana 2009).This is an important moment for the moth-er, as she has to let go of her son, into something of which she has no knowledge and no experience. While in the bush the boys live in round huts (*amaboma*) that have been prepared for them. During holiday periods one can see, even in urban areas near the highways, makeshift huts with their tied-together plastic sheeting. The initiates (*abakhwetha*), whom one can recognize by their white-painted faces, are accompanied by traditional attendants (*amakhankatha*), whose responsibility it is to nurse the wounds and supervise the young men. The traditional surgeon, called the *ingcibi*, is usually chosen by the boy's father. This is important as it ensures involvement of the father and his family. If there is no paternal involvement, things could go horribly wrong, as was the case with Mgqolozana. The first week away is the beginning of the seclusion period; there is the settling in and preparation for the circumcision. There seems to be variation in this: in Mgqolazana's case the circumcision happened straight after the nighttime vigil—right at the beginning of the process. More often the first week is an introductory period.

The purpose of this significant ritual is to make the boy into a man—concretely this is done by the circumcision and all that follows, but the boys are also given instructions about what it means to be a man and how they should henceforth conduct themselves. This important component is often neglected in modern times, and its neglect is a significant loss for the young men and ultimately for society as a whole. Various rules apply during this time, to which both the traditional surgeon and the boys have to adhere, one of the most important being that no contact with any woman is allowed. There is also a way of speaking in metaphors that only those who have been through this process can understand, and it is taboo to share these or give them away to the uninitiated.

The entire rite culminates in the circumcision itself. Traditionally this was done with an assegai or a very sharp knife. Today surgical blades are increasingly being used. On completion of the circumcision the *ingcibi* calls out *Yithi uyindoda*, "You are a man," to which the boy replies *Ndiyindoda*, "I am a man." This is the moment he has been waiting for all his life and marks his change of status from child to adult man. Then follows a phase of intense pain and hardship: the wound is raw and bleeding; traditional medicines are applied and it is bandaged in a prescribed manner. No drinking of water or any fluids is allowed, and no eating of ordinary food—only so-called hard food is allowed. This consists of kernels of maize called *inkobe*. This is of course completely contrary to what is physically needed—especially during the summer months when dehydration is a real possibility. This difficult and "hard" period lasts for eight days and ends with the *umojiso* ceremony: a goat or sheep is slaughtered in celebration of the healing of the wound; only now is eating ordinary food again permitted.

The boys remain in the bush for a variable period—from three weeks to one month. In previous times this was much longer and could last up to six months; however with modern schooling requirements, this is no longer possible, and an abbreviated period is acceptable. The termination of seclusion is marked by the dismantling of the huts and sometimes the old clothes being burned. On reaching home the young men, now known as *amarkhwala,* are greeted with jubilation and a great feast. They receive new clothes and a new blanket. Traditionally they are meant to obey certain codes of conduct for a few months. From this time onward everyone in the family, including the mother, treats the son with the respect and distance that a man traditionally receives.

Recounting his childhood in Upper Guinea in *The African Child,* Camara Laye (1954) describes an interesting variation of this ritual. Here an additional element of fear is introduced: before the actual circumcision the boys have to endure a night in the wilderness where they are exposed to the roar of Konden Diara—a mythical lion about which they have been told since their early childhood. The boys have to manage their terror and thereafter have to endure the physical pain of the circumcision. The point of this is to learn to "sink low" and to endure pain, because this is one of the most important preparations for life. Life is not expected to be free of hardship and thus pain is not avoided, as in Europe, but is faced and endured; the preparation for this starts early in childhood (A. Nyamende, pers. comm., 2002). Mgqolozana conveys the experience firsthand: "The circumcision process is a physical and tangible manifestation of what manhood is really about. It teaches you how to endure, how to manoeuvre your way through and out of difficult situations that life presents to you. It trains you in the lessons of patience, for it is something that cannot be rushed through but can only be completed step by step" (Mgqolozana 2009, 65).

A Rite of Transition into Manhood

In 1909 the French scholar Arnold van Gennep published his most famous work regarding rites of passage ceremonies (van Gennep 1960). Rites are found in all societies and are particularly evident during transition stages in the life cycle. Even in western societies such rites exist, such as the bar mitzvah and confirmation. Three phases are generally found in the *rites de passage:* separation, transition, and incorporation. The relative weight given to each varies from one culture and rite to another. In the *ukoluka* all three are strongly manifest. During the separation it is the task to detach from all that is known. The boy has to bid farewell to his mother and she to him. This is a very real good-bye, a time of tremendous anguish for mothers; they enter states of deep anxiety as they do not know whether their sons will return undamaged or even return alive.

Turner (1987) considers in depth the middle phase of transition or liminality. He regards this marginal period as the time in which the transformation of the person occurs. It is an in-between stage, one of dissolution accompanied by growth. It is also the most challenging part of the whole *ukoluka* ritual—having to survive physical pain, hunger, and deprivation. The boy is not allowed to regress to an infantile stage; he cannot withdraw and find comfort. He must consciously endure the pain and hardship, and in Upper Guinea he has to overcome his fear, because this is what becoming a man entails. The reunion and reincorporation into the community are the final phase—the one called "aggregation." The boy has become a man, and he appears dressed in new clothes and is greeted with great joy by all, particularly the women. The event is accompanied by a great celebration.

A man who has not been to the bush is not regarded as a proper man, and this holds true not only in the rural, more traditional areas but also in the cities, where young men with tertiary education do not see themselves as full men unless they have gone through this process. "No self-respecting Xhosa girl would marry a Xhosa male unless he had submitted to . . . the Xhosa circumcision ritual" (Crowley and Kesner 1990, 318). A field study done in 1998 found that among those young men interviewed there was overwhelming support for the ritual; only six out of seventy-six people objected to its practice or had reservations (Meintjies 1998). This is close to 80 percent support. The alternative of a hospital circumcision is not an option because it "is a medical procedure [that is] not a culturally significant event in a man's life and it takes away the value of circumcision as indicative of a man's worth in his group. The various physical hardships endured by the initiates strengthen them so as to be able to resist the evil influences in their life ahead" (Funani 1990, 56). The fact that women—that is, the nurses—are then also involved in the procedure would go against the whole thrust of this rite of passage and would be its undoing.

A question arising is why this tradition continues with such strength in modern society, despite opposition from numerous quarters because of medical complications and fatalities (Meissner and Buso 2007). The rich symbolism of the *ukoluka* is embedded within and comes out of a lived family and community context, one that has remained essentially unchanged; this is what gives it meaning and cultural weight.

Mother and Father in Traditional and Modern African Society

In traditional Africa growing up means being close to the mother; the baby is breastfed on demand for the first eighteen months or so of life. This is borne out by an observation done on an African mother-infant dyad in Cape Town, which recorded the following: "The presence of the mother's body and mind was constant, day and night, and the continuous availability of the breast prevented early experiences of discontinuity" (Maiello 2000, 88).

The baby sleeps with his mother until such time as he is ready, of his own accord, to go to sleep with his siblings; he is carried on his mother's back for as long as he is not able to walk. For the mother this is what parenting is all about and she does not complain about any of these tasks. When asked whether a two-year-old toddler (who was disabled and hence could not walk) was not too heavy for his mother to carry, the reply was a Xhosa saying: "Does the elephant complain about his trunk?" The infant is a part of her and there is no anxiety, no complaining around this; it is something to which she can give herself fully. The separation occurs gradually and almost imperceptibly. In sharp contrast, multiple anxieties and doubts can fill the European mother's mind about where her baby should sleep, when she should wean him from the breast, and so forth.

The role of the father is far more variable. We have to separate out what was tradition and what has changed as a result of the various factors that have impacted the indigenous family: the effects of western imperialism, the policy of Apartheid, and now increasing urbanization and globalization. The original family still exists in the more isolated rural areas of the country: Through the tradition of *lobola* or bridewealth, the woman becomes part of the man's family. The husband is obliged to provide her with a homestead and lifelong security; all children born belong to the husband's family and clan (Preston-Whyte 1937). There is thus an in-built security not only between the couple but also between the two families.

In most traditional families the father is not involved in infant care—for as long as infants are physically dependent on the mother, the father stays on the outside of the relationship. As a boy gets older he plays with other boys, and through them he learns how to herd the cattle and how to fight with sticks and wooden spears (van der Vliet 1974). His first proper entry into the world of his father and the men of his clan is when he goes through the initiation process.

This ordered way of living has changed dramatically: what was started by colonization was continued and solidified under Apartheid. Traditional forms of leadership were undermined; African men were used in subservient roles to work for white-owned enterprises; they were separated from their families, who were not allowed to join them in the white cities. Colonialism and Apartheid transformed existing masculinities and created new ones (Morrell 1998). Men then took a second wife in the city, and another family came into being. A new form of male identity also emerged during this time—the *indlavini* is a man characterized by violent behavior, recklessness, and disrespect toward the elders and their traditions (Mkhize 2004). And thus the seeds were sown for the situation we have today—men who have little idea of duty and responsibility, who father children but do not live with them. In post-Apartheid South Africa fathers live with their biological children in only two out of five households (Barbarin and Richter 2001, 143).

This gloomy statistic is borne out by clinical experience: during the fifteen years of community work in the township of Khayelitsha, we have seen few fathers involved with their children or supportive of the mothers. The rupture of the family is evident. This plus the poor quality of education have been some of the causes for many of South Africa's present ills, affecting men in particular, and this in turn has affected the way in which they relate or do not relate to their children.

Modern and particularly urban existence have thus led to the disintegration of family life, even leaving aside the tragedy that death through HIV/AIDS brings. Many men do not even acknowledge their fatherhood; they are not supportive financially, and many are abusive toward the mother and her children. This sad fact has resulted in the Human Sciences Research Council in South Africa initiating the Fatherhood Project (http://www.hsrc.ac.za/fatherhood/index.html),which aims to recognize, encourage, and support men's care and protection of children. The identity of fatherhood is being debated from a social, moral, and relational perspective as well as a cultural one. Mkhize goes as far as to suggest a "crisis of masculinity" (Mkhize 2006, 194) and urges an engagement with this negative identity in the hope of providing new, positive images of fatherhood.

However, at this point in time and before gradual transformation can take place, the situation remains that mothers and their children form close emotional bonds and close bodily attachments. This has remained unchanged from time immemorial. On a psychological level it means that the son stays within the ambit of the mother throughout his childhood.

The imperative to move away from the mother is a universal one; otherwise the new offspring would never become an adult. However, we start life being absolutely dependent on the mother. Erich Neumann (1973) writes at length about this early, primal relationship in human beings, stating that the first year of life could be regarded as the extrauterine phase of the embryo's development, such is the closeness, the psychic and physical integration with the mother's body. "The earliest knowing of the world and ego development in and through the body occur in the closest union with the mother, not only with her body which gives nourishment, warmth and protection, but also with the child's whole unconscious love for its mother and the mother's whole conscious and unconscious love for the child and its body" (31).

The complexity of this early interaction contributes to the neuronal growth and extensive wiring that characterize the human brain. If we follow the line of Jean Knox's argument regarding archetypes as psychic patterns, and more specifically as image schemata (Knox 2003), it could be alleged that in past and present African society the child remains in the image schema of the circle, the container, for a long time.

In a patriarchal society it is particularly important for the boy not only to move away from the mother but to move toward and identify with the father and the males of his clan. This move from the matriarchate to the patriarchate is a formidable task—and is reflected in many writings in analytical psychology. Jung's theorizing on this is contained in his *Symbols of Transformation,* the work in which he set himself apart from Freud and classical psychoanalysis (Jung 1976). Every chapter has to do with a different aspect of this enormous challenge of separating from the mother and staying separate from her. "The Battle of Deliverance from the Mother" is the title of the chapter following those that describe the birth of the hero. To become a hero is one accomplishment; to stay on the heroic journey requires another ongoing battle. To be delivered from the mother psychologically speaking, even after physical separation, is no small feat.

Freud too based a large part of his work on this struggle, the Oedipus myth being at its center. He writes: "A human being's first choice of an object is regularly an incestuous one, aimed, in the case of a male, at his mother and sister; and it calls for the severest prohibitions to deter this persistent infantile tendency from realization" (Freud 1974, 378). The incest taboo runs deep in human nature, and only the ancient gods were accorded the right to have relationships within their families. There is of course a good scientific reason why this is not advisable for humans: if it were not for this taboo the species would ultimately not survive. To retreat back to the mother or sister is the easiest route to take, but biologically it would result in progressive restriction of the gene pool. In mythology it is thus not surprising that castration, the most severe form of punishment, is the result of the enactment of this wish.

Jung posits the notion that the hero myth is born out of the human need to become an individual, separate from the parents, particularly the mother. The hero's task is to resist his infantile impulses and wishes of returning to and uniting with the mother.

> The regression of libido reactivates the ways and habits of childhood, and above all the relation to the mother; but what was natural and useful to the child is a psychic danger for the adult, and this is expressed by the symbol of incest. Because the incest taboo opposes the libido and blocks the path to regression, it is possible for the libido to be canalized into mother analogies thrown up by the unconscious. In that way the libido becomes progressive again, and even attains a level of consciousness higher than before. (Jung 1976, 213)

Metaphorical equivalents referring to the mother and symbols representing aspects of the mother thus become possible, and indeed become a necessity, otherwise this blocked libido has nowhere to go. The urge to return to the mother is depicted in numerous myths and human activities. An interesting African mother analogy originating from Zimbabwe is the custom of binding the ash of wood coming from the ancestral homestead tree with egg white and smearing this on the fontanel of the newborn baby (T. J. Tapela, pers. comm., 2005). This functions as a protection for the child. We can see in this how the use of the tree, well known as a mother symbol, takes the place of the maternal womb to shield the most vulnerable part of the infant from outside harm.

Besides finding mother analogies and symbols to substitute for the actual mother, the resolution of the Oedipal complex is through identification with the father and the world of men. The hypothesis here is that, generally speaking and coming from personal observation, non-westernized African mothers are able to give themselves over to the primal union with a child without anxiety as they know, consciously or unconsciously, that when the time is right, their sons will be separated from them and that the incest taboo will thereby be respected. Even if the biological father is absent, a male member of the father's clan (or the mother's clan) will take it upon himself to be involved in the child's *ukoluka* ritual and make sure it is done in the proper manner.

The Battle for Deliverance from the Mother

Human beings have since their very beginning attempted to give meaning to life and to ensure that the group not only survives but betters itself and flourishes. The adolescent rite of passage described here is one of these ways of guaranteeing the physical and mental health of the clan. It is a ritual that is "symbolically saturated" (Vincent 2008, 434), and analytical psychology provides useful ways in which the symbols can be understood. This rite of passage contains elements of the hero myth. "The process of masculinization finally crystallizes out at this point and proves to be decisive for the structure of ego consciousness" (Neumann 1954, 131). Within the broad frame of the hero's journey, several archetypal themes and images are constellated through this ritual.

To start with the image schema of the archetype: the move from the soft, round circle of the mother to the hard, angular "weapon" of the father is embedded in many of the details of this rite. First, contact is only with men—any "soft" option of being mothered or nursed by a female is prohibited; hence the tragedy when circumcision goes wrong and hospitalization is required. Then there is the weapon of the *ingcibi* with which the circumcision is performed, followed by the difficult stage when only hard food is eaten, no fluids are imbibed, and severe pain is endured. No soft, round figure comes to the rescue, offering digestible food and milk; the only mother analogy possibly present is the *amaboma*, the round huts, into which initiates retreat. This could be seen as a temporary regression into the womb in order to be strengthened and reborn.

If we now extend the image schema to a more complex symbolic level, we come to a host of archetypally based motifs. While van Gennep regarded circumcision as a mutilation, he did consider it a means of "permanent differentiation"—boys from men (van Gennep 1960, 74).

Jung takes matters to a deeper plane with the notion of sacrifice and describes the cult legend of Attis (Jung 1976). Attis is driven insane by the love of Cybele, his mother, and he castrates himself under a pine tree. Cybele's followers commemorate this legendary deed by the annual felling of a pine tree. Jung explains at length the double meaning of the tree—standing for both the mother and the son's phallus. The felling is the castration, on the one hand, denoting the sacrifice of the libido, but it at the same time it stands for the "killing" of the mother and, through that, the attainment of libido. The intertwining of double meanings within this one act makes this a deeply meaningful ritual and clearly demonstrates the immense power of symbolic castration.

Jung goes on to write about sacrifice: "The essence and motive force of the sacrificial drama consists in an unconscious transformation of energy." (Jung 1976, 429), and "By sacrificing . . . the instinctive desire, or libido, is given up in order that it may be regained in new form. Through sacrifice man ransoms himself from the fear of death" (431). The transformation of energy is needed whenever there is a change of status for the individual in society. Going away is bidding farewell to childhood, in particular to the mother, and this is the task of the young adult male. During this period the mother suffers greatly—her fear for her son's well-being, indeed for his survival, is real and can probably be equated to the feeling of sending him into battle. She literally has to give him up, sacrifice him, and he literally has to leave her behind. As the original attachment between mother and son was experienced so immediately on a bodily level, so this separation is an enactment on a physical level. Connected with sacrifice is also the motif of death and rebirth—again, very concretely, there is the danger that he will not make it; and even if the boy does not die, he may come home mutilated, and this could be worse than death.

The myth that is being played out is classically that of the hero: the boy exposes himself to danger for the purpose of attaining a higher goal. The giving up of the foreskin, paradoxically endangering the boy's manhood, symbolizes the letting go of childhood and specifical-ly the mother. He has to confront that which he fears most, and thus he becomes "both the sacrificer and the sacrificed" (Jung 1976, 428). Neumann richly describes how the hero needs to overcome his fear of castration, which is "man's immemorial fear of woman" (Neumann 1954, 156). Of interest to note is that the eighth-day circumcision in Judaism marks the time when the infant is said to move symboli-cally from the mother to the father—a sign of a patriarchal culture (Dreifuss 1965). However, it could be argued that this has little to do with the infant boy's willing or conscious separation from his mother and more to do with the collective symbol of a people belonging to-gether and sharing a particular Father-God.

The severance from the mother's world, from the childhood home, the living among men in the bush and surviving on minimal means with no comforts, marks entrance into the world of the adult male. This is accompanied, to a greater or lesser degree depending on the group's tradition, with discussions and instructions regarding sexual practices and the expected conduct of a man in his particular clan. It may be regarded as the time when father and son truly connect. From a western perspective it could be said that whatever may have been missing regarding fatherly involvement during early childhood is now compensated for in an intense manner. The desired Oedipal identification with the father and his world is taking place now; how-ever, it must be remembered that knowledge of this process is present in the cultural unconscious of the boy and his family from his birth, so that what happens in late adolescence is merely an actualization of what was expected all along.

With the putting on of new clothes and the return to festivities and celebration in the home, the circle is closed. The motif of death and re-birth has been constellated, particularly for both mother and son. Her boy has died and a man has returned, and in future she treats him with the respect a man deserves. Is there anything in western culture that could match the certainty and incisiveness of this African tradition?

So, What about Traditions?

Separation and development away from the mother, the primary love object, is a universal human necessity and is particularly challenging for the boy child. The Oedipal situation requires a resolution, which cultures have provided for in their different ways. I suggest that as long as fathers are on the periphery of their infants' care and upbring-ing, the unconscious will ensure that a rite of passage literally cutting the tie to the mother will prevail and retain its power. It is not for anyone to condemn an ancient tradition that has a specific and deep function; rather we need understanding as to why it remains so pow-erfully present.

This culture will gradually change with time, as all cultures do; it may be that as the sciences reveal the importance of the begin-ning of life, fathers may choose to become more involved with their young children's early development; perhaps then this tradition may not be required in its original form and may undergo modification or even spontaneously wane. But then it will be on the basis of an archetypal imperative having been heeded; that is, it will come from deep below, from the double bass of the orchestral score, which would then influence the manner in which the first violin plays the theme. Trying to force it the other way round, which is what the cur-rent danger is for indigenous cultures confronted with modern laws and ways, could have serious repercussions for the collective psyche of a people. And what could be more devastating than loss of soul?

While change and evolution are inherent to all cultures, the striv-ing toward the western model as a better one needs to be questioned. In the African context this is of particular relevance as the coloniza-tion of the people and their land by European powers has had such devastating consequences. The adolescent rite of passage performed by large groups in South Africa is currently under particular scrutiny, and there are calls for it to be done away with or changed.

The ritual of circumcision nonetheless continues to be widespread. Through the theoretical lens of analytical psychology this ritual can be viewed in its depth, and the consequent resistance to it being abolished can be more fully appreciated. When an archetypal imperative is being fulfilled, in this case the separation between mother and son, then surface arguments are not likely to make an impression. Only once the archetypal imperative has been met in a different manner could a change in the practice be forthcoming. The wisdom from which traditional worldviews spring needs to be acknowledged; one hopes the attitudes coming from a western perspective may then become less·elevated and more respectful.

CHAPTER 6

Ubuntu

AN AFRICAN CONTRIBUTION TO THE "CIVILIZATION AS A WHOLE"

If you have two cows, and the milk of the first cow is enough for your own consumption, ubuntu expects you to donate the milk of the second cow to your underprivileged brother and sister.
—Walter Sisulu, 1993

These words spoken by Walter Sisulu (Broodryk 2002, 13) give us a clear picture of what being human is all about: that of which we have enough we should offer to those who are in need. This is *ubuntu*. It is not demanding that we should give if we do not have; it merely asks that we share. This injunction seems straightforward enough, but it nonetheless requires careful analysis.

Ubuntu comes from the African proverb *Umntu ngumntu ngabantu,* which literally translated means "a person is a person because of persons." "I am because you are" is another way of expressing this. Personhood and individuation are thus firmly situated within the context of human relationships. We are all part of one another, and what affects one person affects all of us. Archbishop Tutu regards this interdependence among people as the essence of being human: "It speaks of the fact that my humanity is caught up and inextricably bound up in yours. I am human because I belong" (Tutu 2005, 26). It is the very fabric of humanity; the way being in the world is experienced and lived. Researchers such as Daniel Stern, working with infants, would no doubt agree with this wholeheartedly; for the baby there is no self without an other (Stern 1985). Though Stern is still very much in the mode of the dyad—the twosome, self and other—what ubuntu implies is self and others, in the plural, and it may well be ahead of its time in terms of not limiting itself to one other; infant research has shown that from an early age, babies are able to connect simultaneously with more than one person (von Klitzing et al. 1999).

Behind the ordinariness and simplicity of this idea there is a hidden complexity. In this chapter I aim to unpack and differentiate some of the nuances of this African concept. From a European perspective there are two major challenges bound up with conveying the sense of ubuntu. First, it is more than a theory; it is a way of being, even a way of feeling, that defies description. It is a lived experience to which one has to be exposed in order to grasp it truly. L. J. Sebidi reflects on the difficulty in defining ubuntu and states that it is a "non-perceptible, almost un-definable, quality or attribute of human acts the presence or absence of which can only be intuited by the human mind" (in Mnyaka 2003, 143). Through the descriptions offered in this chapter I hope some of this undefinable quality will come into view. Second, as a concept it is difficult if not impossible to place within the western, known model of the mind. I have previously described it in terms of a "cultural complex" (Berg 2004). On further reflection some years later, I realize that this category does not do justice to ubuntu, and I shall explain why this could be so.

The term *cultural complex* gained ascendancy through a book with that title (Singer and Kimbles 2004). The authors describe the cultural complex as being the result of "repetitive, historical group experiences which have taken root in the cultural unconscious of the group. At any ripe time, these . . . take hold of the collective psyche of the group and the individual" (Singer and Kimbles 2004, 7). Through exploring this particular type of complex an attempt is made to find a way to explain group and cultural conflict, that "which tears us apart"'" (1). The implicit hope is that by having a deeper understanding of one another's cultural complexes, we can find resolution to conflict. As will be seen, ubuntu does not match this description, and yet I previously tailored it in such a way that it could become a cultural complex. The question is why I tried so hard to do that. Why did I make such a serious attempt to fit an African concept and an African experience into a model that comes from another continent?

There was of course a wish to make what I was describing understandable to the westernized reader; ubuntu is such a special attribute that I was keen for all to be able to grasp it and thought that if it fitted into a commonly accepted category, it would be more readily shareable. However, there is more to it than that—it seems that unless something is articulated in terms of the dominant culture, unless it is made congruent with a recognized notion or concept, it does not really exist. Only by giving it generally understood, western labels, does it become legitimate and something that really is there.

But perhaps times are changing; perhaps there may be a turnaround, an enantiodromia; perhaps developing countries are gathering a sense of identity and dare to offer what is their own; that which cannot be forced into direct translation. And perhaps things do exist, even if they defy western categories. The well-known poet, writer, and journalist Antjie Krog struggles with these issues too and is frustrated by these "assumed understandings and non-understandings"; she writes the following when she tries to articulate the African world view of ubuntu:

Nothing can be said in the world that the West has not already said. What I am trying to describe has NOT been grasped by the West, and if you think what I am saying is the same as what these other philosophers [of the West] are saying, then it simply means we from Africa have not yet properly managed to articulate it succinctly. And it is hard: we have to use Western tools. It is as if we have to help you eat *braaivleis* [barbeque] with chopsticks. (Krog 2009a, 156)

Braaivleis has to be eaten with the hands. There is no way that chopsticks will do. So perhaps we have to acknowledge that some cultural concepts stand separate and cannot be forced to fit the western "psychoanalytic self" (Roland 1996). A fundamental *Weltanschauung,* like ubuntu, cannot and indeed should not be reduced in order to fit a framework that originates in another kind of cosmology. In what follows I hope it will become clear why ubuntu stands apart and why it cannot be regarded as being one of the cultural complexes.

Despite this insight, I have continued to struggle against the default tendency to attach categories to the concept of ubuntu. Superficially speaking, ubuntu may appear in various ways, ways that were difficult and indeed impossible to put together. The temptation was to create headings or groupings so that the phenomenology could be fixed: if we could we talk of a personal vs. a transpersonal level, or a concrete and literal vs. abstract and symbolic one, or real vs. defensive use, positive vs. negative, use vs. abuse, etc., then we might be able to pin it down. But then questions arise. Are these truly different positions, different levels on a spectrum of ubuntu, or are they the way in which ubuntu gets used by people, or am I merely trying to find a label that would satisfy my western mindset? After much searching, both in the literature and within my own experience and "felt" knowledge, the conclusion that I reached is that ubuntu itself is without contradictions or polarities. The deep felt sense of this notion is beyond schisms. When these schisms seem to appear, then it is not because of ubuntu itself being fractured but because the word is being used by individuals to suit their personal needs.

Ubuntu and Religion

The nearest theoretical explanation one could have of ubuntu is that it has a deeply religious meaning (Louw 2002) and that because of this it is beyond psychological theorizing. Ultimately "a person is a person because of other persons" links the individual not only to the living but to the ancestors, those in the beyond, those "on the other side." The living and the deceased are connected with one another and dependent on one another. The living remember and revere the dead, and the ancestors in turn act as mentors and guides to the living and ultimately as mediators with the Great Spirit or Creator. Mndende places ubuntu within the moral order of African religion—helping others, sharing with others is a sine qua non of living within a society. The poor should not have to ask for help—the offer should come from the rich, and they should not praise themselves for doing so; that is the prerogative of the person who has been helped (Mndende 2006).

But while ubuntu may fall within the ambit of a religious attitude, this does not imply a fervent religiosity that aims at promulgating itself. Within this African religious attitude there is tolerance and acceptance of other peoples' beliefs. This is not a religion in the way we may understand

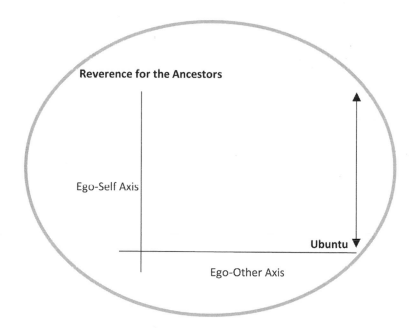

Ancestor reverence and community-oriented ubuntu, the two intersecting axes in African Religion, together constitute an all-encompassing attitude, a way of relating to all fellow human beings.

it. It is not about dogma or the need to convert; it is also not about buildings and structures, towers and bells; it has no sacred texts with commandments, no special days of worship. It is an attitude, a way of living one's life and a way of relating to fellow human beings that is as much part of the person as his or her bone marrow is. It is a part of the heritage of Africa that is implicitly transmitted: whatever needs to be explicitly handed on in terms of rites and ceremonies is conveyed via oral tradition and lived example. Of course, the implicit, genetically encoded transmission cannot occur without a releasing stimulus in the environment—thus a child growing up in a society that is not imbued with this attitude will not automatically acquire it. And this is where the danger of its loss lies—parts of modern Africa may well move so far away from their roots that this very special attribute will become something that sounds good but has lost its real value.

The theologian D. J. Louw shares the view which the writer Antjie Krog articulates: namely, that ubuntu "serves as a distinctly African rationale for . . . ways of relating to others" (Louw 2002, 19). It is an ethical ideal; it is a task and something that still needs to be realized, particularly in the new South Africa, and also in the world at large. Sharing with others is not a new philosophy and it is not a uniquely African one either—but with ubuntu there is something different. It may be the intensity with which it is expressed in Africa; it may have to do with the way it is lived. This is perhaps a somewhat ironic proposal in the light of this continent's severe difficulties with power sharing and its expression of extreme violence. But ubuntu belongs to people, ordinary people; it is on the ground that it is found, and not necessarily in the corridors of power.

Why Ubuntu Is Not a Cultural Complex

Complexes are understood to be autonomous psychic forces, which grab hold of the ego; they "possess a high degree of autonomy" (Jung 1969b, 97). One of the characteristics of a complex activation is that it produces an affective discharge and can often cause people to behave in a manner that is out of keeping with their usual way of behaving. Complexes can be handicapping and can cause distress; often help is sought in order to alleviate this distress. The analysis of complexes and their resolution, or at least reduction, is thus one of the aims of any analytically oriented psychotherapy. Activated cultural complexes are characterized by intense collective emotions that spring from collective, often historical, group experiences. Like personal complexes, they tend to be bipolar (Singer and Kimbles 2004). Ubuntu is not something that grabs hold of the person or group in an autonomous way, nor is it a "splinter psyche" (Jung 1969b, 97) that overwhelms the ego and causes it to feel and do things that are out of the ordinary for that person. In fact, it is the very opposite—those people who have lost their ubuntu are regarded as having lost their humanity. Ubuntu is also not bipolar—if there is a negative aspect, it is not because of the notion itself having a negative component; rather it is because human beings misuse it.

I propose that ubuntu finds expression in multiple ways, some more personal, lived through day-to-day interactions, and others transpersonal in that they include the other in a more collective sense. However, the desire to be with and work with the other is the basis, as the saying "One finger cannot pick up a grain" so beautifully depicts; it starts from the personal and extends to the beyond to embrace the stranger and the whole of humanity in the way that Tutu has suggested. Without ubuntu South Africa would not have had the smooth transition to democracy that occurred. In fact, it explicitly formed part of the interim constitution formulated in 1994.

At the end of this document, under the heading "National Unity and Reconciliation," the following appears:

> The adoption of this Constitution lays the secure foundation for the people of South Africa to transcend the divisions and strife of the past, which generated gross violations of human rights, the transgression of humanitarian principles in violent conflicts and a legacy of hatred, fear, guilt and revenge.
>
> These can now be addressed on the basis that there is a need for understanding but not for vengeance, a need for reparation but not for retaliation, a need for ubuntu but not for victimisation. (*Constitution* 1993).

That the word *ubuntu* is specifically included is significant and truly gives this document an African flavor.

And on April 27, 1994, we realized what so many hoped for: an exhilaratingly peaceful day of voting made us all equal, one and the same. The relief and joy were indescribable—we could look one another in the eye, for the first time. It was a splendid beginning and would not have been possible without the spirit of ubuntu suffusing many parts of the country.

This feeling, this sense of being together, was palpable—and still is palpable—to those who live and also those who visit parts of South Africa, irrespective of increasing urbanization and westernized education. It is felt on the ground, in day-to-day interactions with ordinary people, more than among politicians, who unfortunately speak about it more than actually living it. The term has also come to be used in an over-inclusive and self-serving manner. It has found its way into advertising, business management, and the like. The danger of course is that its real meaning may get diluted, mixed up and lost, resulting in it becoming stereotyped and clichéd. However, the very fact that the term remains alive attests to its continued appeal and proves that in it is contained an essence that continues to be meaningful and vital.

Very early into the new South Africa I had an experience that gave me this felt sense *of ubuntu*. It occurred while I was walking in the township of Khayelitsha. The year was 1995, just after the first election. I was rather anxious and ill at ease, as these were new surroundings for me. I wrote about it at the time:

> I recall one Tuesday morning in the beginning when I was walking with my co-worker, Nosisana Nama, along the street, one side of which had shops selling all sorts of things—from meat to clothes to taped music. On the other side was a children's creche and a little boy was peering over the wall, calling out something in Xhosa. I heard a man on the opposite side shouting back at him and the child ducked. I was told that the little boy had exclaimed, "Look, a white woman." The man had chided him, saying, "She is your mother." (Berg 2002b, 104)

This interaction moved me deeply—here was this older man, who had known the inhumanity of Apartheid from which we were just emerging, but who was accepting me as a person and teaching this young child to do the same. In African tradition anyone who could be another person's parent in terms of age is addressed with the respectful term of *uMama* or *uTata*. He was telling the child not to look at skin color but at the position of the person in terms of age, and to act accordingly. This older gentleman was not seized by an autonomous part of his psyche that made him act out of character—he was completely himself, calm, confident, and spoke to this child in a completely natural manner. And probably most persons of his generation would have done the same, or at least felt the same, even if they had kept quiet or reacted in a different way. There is much to learn for us in the western, so-called civilized world.

This is more than old-fashioned good manners—it goes beyond mere outer personal civility. It is a way of relating and interacting that is difficult to capture in words. But to call this a complex is a violation—it is like forcing a sense of being into concrete shape; by giving it a psychological (in fact, psychopathological) name, we reduce it. Perhaps if we place the two different worldviews next to each other—the European and the African—we can light up other facets of this simple but layered and nuanced notion.

I Think, Therefore I Am

The western northern hemisphere is probably regarded as the center of rationality and progress in the modern world. But Europe was not always a progressive and rational place. During the Middle Ages superstitions abounded; the Roman Catholic Church was the authority on all matters pertaining to living and dying—those who dared to counter its views were admonished and even executed. Galileo, for example, escaped death only because he recanted his theory regarding the position of the earth in the solar system.

Descartes, who was born thirty years after Galileo and who ushered in the period of Enlightenment, came from a position of radical doubt (Auerbach and Blatt 2001). He refused simply to believe and took the opposite position: he doubted his senses because of their subjective nature, he doubted the very existence of his own body— the only thing he could not doubt was that he was doubting; that is, that he was thinking. Further diminution was not possible, and thus he stayed with the statement *cogito ergo sum*. This ability to think is the barest minimum, the simplest fact of our human existence, and proves that we "are."

The taking apart and examining of the component bits individually was the beginning of objective science. Not only was being human condensed to an essence; so was the physical world examined under a microscope, leading to major discoveries, such as the discovery of micro-organisms, like those causing tuberculosis, and from there cures were found. The tremendous advantages coming out of scientific discourse and discoveries are obvious. The logical, step-by-step buildup of reasoning, where point B follows point A in a straight line, can be seen by everybody and can be proven—there is reliability and validity.

The development of industry, medicine, and technology could not have occurred without this way of thinking. It has led to progress, which has led to wealth, which has led to luxury. These advances, which have such obvious outer manifestations, have become equated with well-being; those who have this know-how within their grasp have come to immense power. Everybody would like to live a long life in comfort and security, and it is not surprising that most human beings on this earth would wish to have a share in this.

Logic, rationality, and the premium given to the individual have become the dominant part of the western psyche and lifestyle. We no longer need the other to ensure our survival—if we have the means, we can ensure health and prosperity. Hence this way of viewing the world has become the golden standard by which quality of life is defined. However, it also means that this way of viewing the world has acquired a hypertrophied, overgrown "muscle," with which it assumes superiority over other cultures whose values and traditions are different.

Wolfgang Giegerich expands and amplifies on his understanding of modern man's state or level of consciousness in his "The End of Meaning and the Birth of Man" (Giegerich 2004). In this essay he goes to great lengths, and uses many persuasive analogies, to prove that modern man has emerged from "the ocean of meaning" (19), and indeed if he has not, he ought to emerge from the womb provided by mythology and the need for meaning. Giegerich argues that modern man has no choice but to insist on "emancipated individuality and rationality." This is a deeply modern European view, which Giegerich has every right to represent and defend. However, it cannot be assumed that "modern man" or modern consciousness in the way he describes it applies to the whole of humanity. In Africa and in other parts of the nonwestern world different impulses, different values are alive and want to find expression. And this does not necessarily mean that modern western people are is more advanced than African or Indian people.

The assumed superiority of the West has been present ever since the first European set foot on African soil. Jung himself was not shy to make the claim of his consciousness being the vehicle for recognition "that this was the world" (Jung 1963, 284), thereby implying that other human beings who must also have stood on this hill in Kenya did not really count because he was the first truly "conscious" man to stand there. Throughout Jung's account of his travels in Africa there is the sense that he knew better; however, at the same time, he feared the "primitive" in the African people; he was terrified of the "wild horde" (301) that could be unleashed with a dancing episode. His dream of the Negro making his hair kinky awoke in him a sense of alarm. While Jung had respect and admiration for what he saw as the Negro's wholeness, he nevertheless continued with the "layered" model of the psyche, which was the accepted view of the time. That is, the upper, modern layer belongs to the white psyche, and the black psyche has only the lower layers.

If we were to continue along those lines, we run into the problem of a quantitative comparison: who has more of what? White Europe has more civilization than black Africa? Black Africans are closer to their instincts than Europeans? The need to show superiority can only mean that there is an unconscious inferiority. Let difference rather be examined dispassionately, and may respect flow from that. Now in the twenty-first century with its increasingly dangerous polarities emerging, it behooves us to understand and meet each other on equal terms.

Africa did not break down the human body and mind into small parts to be examined individually. Africa followed another path, one where whole beings remained intact within their universe. Meaning is all around, in nature, in the happenings to the body, and in dreams, which are taken seriously. Rituals can help if the balance is upset and things go wrong. These rituals involve the body and mind, which are not split.

A surprising example of respect for this other path comes from a relatively unknown source named John Vernon Taylor, who was the general secretary of the Church Missionary Society for ten years from 1963 and was bishop of Winchester for the next decade. He wrote many books, one being *The Primal Vision* (Taylor 1963). In this work he seeks to establish the essentially African way of perceiving the world. While his ultimate aim was to equip him to meet with African people in order to talk to them about Christianity from their point of view, it would serve the European-oriented psychotherapist in Africa well to peruse this small book. We owe to Taylor the paraphrasing of Descartes to "I participate, therefore I am."

Taylor is at pains to emphasize that the notion of the "primitive" so often applied to African thinking, including as we have already seen by Jung, is a misnomer, as it implies an evolutionary perspective and movement toward a higher, more developed state. Taylor quotes Levy-Bruhl as initially having classified this way of thinking as "pre-logical" but later having conceded that the logical structure of the human mind is the same in all people (Taylor 1963, 30). Taylor is emphatic that an African is as competent to understand and enter into the complexities of European or any other thought as the European is of entering the African *Weltanschauung*, given the correct attitude. My personal clinical experience with long-term analyses of patients of black African origin amply confirms this.

According to Taylor, one of the fundamental differences between European thinking and African thinking is the location of the self—that which defines the "I," consciousness, that which is inside and outside "me." In the traditional European way of thinking, dreams come from the inside of a person. In Africa the important dreams come from without, usually from the ancestors. Taylor refers to our definitions of the ego and the id, dreams and fantasies, which we regard as being confined to the individual's mind: "We are in danger of forgetting that all this is only a figurative way of speaking. The spatial concepts of inside and outside cannot be used literally of something so elusive and abstract as the self; yet in Europe we have allowed them so to dominate our imagery that we have almost identified the mind with the brain and imprisoned the self within the walls of the skull" (44).

Jung was the first psychoanalytic thinker to talk about an objective psyche, a psyche not embedded only within the boundaries of the individual but one that has an existence independent of personal history and memories: " the hidden treasure upon which mankind ever and anon has drawn, and from which it has raised up its gods and demons, and all those potent and mighty thoughts without which man ceases to be man" (Jung 1917, 67).

This links most closely to the African way of being, where there is a more fluid boundary between inner and outer, where the concreteness of outer things can influence the fate of the individual. To draw from Taylor again:

Any attempt to look upon the world through African eyes must involve this adventure of the imagination whereby we abandon our image of a man whose complex identity is encased within the shell of his physical being, and allow ourselves instead to visualize a centrifugal selfhood, equally complex, interpermeating other selves in a relationship in which subject and object are no longer distinguishable. "I think, therefore I am" is replaced by "I participate, therefore I am." (Taylor 1963, 49–50)

Taylor is in part referring to ubuntu, although he does not use the term. His ability to be open and to look at the world through another lens is to be applauded and is an example worth following.

Before giving illustrations of ubuntu, it is worthwhile to speculate as to how this attitude originated, which in turn could throw light on why it is still so alive on the continent of Africa.

Possible Origins of Ubuntu

It is a given that from the very beginning of life all babies need a caregiver; through this primary need, they come into relationship from the start. No development of the self is possible without a concomitant appreciation of and a relationship to the other. This holds for all human infants—it is a universal need that has always been there and is not new. It has merely been researched and made conscious in modern times. It could thus be argued that ubuntu may start off here, on the individual level, for all human beings, and that we are all born into becoming a person through other persons. In some cultures this sense of being through others attenuates, while in other cultures it gets amplified and expands.

Africa is known to be the cradle of humankind. However, we have traditionally regarded Europe and the Middle East as the Old World, the location where modern civilization began—Africa was considered to be a cultural backwater, a place that may have given rise to humanity but did not nurture our later development. This view has been challenged by anthropologists Sally McBrearty and Alison Brooks. They contend that the fully developed signature of modern behavior was present in the African Late Stone Age—long before it was evident in Europe (McBrearty and Brooks 2000). They reach this conclusion via findings that have been made. Pigment use, engravings, bone tools, and personal ornaments support an early emergence of symbolism, these discoveries contradicting the usual notion that Africans were behaviorally primitive. It is thus put forward that modernity in the archaeological sense comes from this continent, as the timing of these objects significantly predates their dispersal out of Africa (d'Errico et al. 2000).

On the basis of these findings it has been suggested that modern humans appear to have exited Africa to populate the rest of the globe only after they had acquired their physical and cognitive abilities (Tattersall 2009). For early humankind daily life was a challenge—challenges were posed by dangerous predators and intermittent food shortages. These may have forced our forebears to find cultural solutions to survive; people needed one another. Survival of the self was inextricably linked with the survival of the group.

Unless there was cooperation and a close being with the other, life itself was threatened. The participation, the belonging, the doing with the other were what enabled the human group not only to continue to exist but to progress. "I am a person because of other persons" was not a philosophical, idealized, and reified concept; it was one that was needed on an actual and concrete level. It had to do with survival and could thus belong to the group of the self-preservative instincts.

If the first civilized human group was in Africa, and if what was made in Africa was exported at a later stage, then it may well be that ubuntu too became part of the way of being in Europe and elsewhere. However, with the scientific revolution of the sixteenth century and Descartes' *cogito ergo sum*, the foundation of modern science and modern development was laid. Nature became less threatening, life was more secure with better nutrition and health care, and thus continued existence of the species became increasingly assured. It is possible that dependence on one another was thus no longer needed, and people could turn to their individual needs without endangering the survival of the group. The Cartesian man and woman could then exist separately and independently from the rest of the community and society (Louw 2002).

But Africa followed a different developmental pathway, one that did not make life that much easier. The sense of having to depend on and be there for one another thus continued to prevail. "The values of Ubuntu are supposedly universal of nature but there is a sense of intensity in all these values which is missing in many other cultures. Since it appears as if this lacking of intensity is [a serious moral] phenomenon in many other cultures, it can be stated that other cultures can indeed learn from Africa" (Broodryk 2002, 16).

Ubuntu in the Family

The thesis put forward here is that ubuntu is part of humanity—it is that which enabled us to stay together and progress together. It started off within the human group—the family and the clan—making it possible for people to survive the odds to which nature exposed them. As mastery of nature progressed, this working together was no longer as necessary. However, on a deep level it remained encoded in our genetic makeup and is evident in the needs of human infants. Later on, when independence is achieved, it is not always obvious. Similarly, at a wider level, those groups who are prosperous do not seem to need other groups as much and are not keen to incorporate others into their collective consciousness.

In South Africa there are pockets of both of these possibilities—modern city life offers a westernized lifestyle in every way, but the rural areas are isolated, and working together with others is vital. Old traditions are respected, and this "indigenous world view of intense humanness" (Broodryk 2002, 15) continues to exist where community and the individual are inseparable (Berinyuu 2002). In urban families where western values have become part of the culture this way of being may be less pronounced.

However, despite a diminution or dilution, the sense of obligation to those to whom one is related remains. This has obvious positive consequences, in that the family will protect the individual and be there for him or her at all costs. Family members know they will support, help, and advise their relatives whenever there is a need. For example, a child who has lost both parents is not called an orphan in traditional society, because the child is immediately taken in by relatives, who without question assume the role of mother or father. It is less a question of biological parentage than of having social parents (Meintjies and Giese 2006). The isiXhosa word for orphan, *inkedama,* means being rejected, cast aside, and it can be seen as an indictment of the family allowing this to happen. Even in urbanized families, failure to care for a child who is part of the clan leaves family and individual reputations in the community severely dented.

An individual who is uncaring and selfish is seen as a nonperson—*akangomntu,* someone who has lost humanity, and this is frowned upon by the community (Mnyaka 2003). This censure, this implicit disapproval, may be enough to bring the person back into line and has a correcting, regulating effect on the collective. The net the family provides affords its members immense security. An isolated, alienated individual is not often seen, though of course this is rapidly changing, and the net can no longer be taken for granted.

Ubuntu in and of itself does not have a negative side—but not all people have ubuntu within them, and some may make use of it in others. Its abuse is often seen in families where there is rivalry: the family member who has succeeded is envied, and demands are made on that person to share what has been earned with the rest of the extended family, thereby ensuring that all live in the same comfort. This often leaves the successful person in a considerable dilemma as what to do, as the sense of obligation to the other is deep.

Ubuntu is then used as an excuse, and the expectation for provision is simply put on the other, without individuals taking responsibility for their situation. However, if ubuntu were present in all, then this selfishness would most certainly be frowned upon (Mnyaka 2003). The sense of responsibility toward others is as great for the one who receives as for the one who gives, and this imperative would be the best protection against misuse. Unfortunately in many families ubuntu is not equally distributed; this puts those who have it in an often intolerable position. It may force them to think in a more western way and draw the line, not giving as freely as they might have if the traditional checks and balances had still been in place.

Lived Ubuntu

Four examples of ubuntu coming from the ground upward, so to speak, illustrate how often and on how many levels its essence is still present. The first has to do with making a space for grieving in what should be an impossible situation; the second is a spontaneous utterance coming from a young mother attending the community clinic; the third originates from a bereaved mother who appeared in front of the Truth and Reconciliation Commission (TRC) in 1996; and the last comes from the person best known in the world for his ubuntu, Nelson Mandela.

Baby P and her mother are both HIV positive. Baby P was so ill that when she was brought to us at the age of five months she weighed less than a newborn baby. Baby and mother were so weak that we thought we would not see them alive again. However, they not only survived but gained in strength as the weeks and months went by.

At the time of writing Baby P is fourteen months old, still small, but able to stand, crawl, and vocalize, and her mother too looks fuller and much stronger. The father, mother's boyfriend, is in all likelihood HIV positive as well but is refusing to be tested and treated—the need to deny is powerful. In the meantime the father had started another relationship, from which a child was born; at the age of ten months this child died, presumably of an HIV-related illness. Although the father and the dead child's mother are no longer a couple, the father asked Baby P's mother to move out of her home so that he and the ex-girlfriend, together with her family, could go through the ritual of burying their child. Baby P's mother agreed and moved out.

Two weeks later we asked how she felt about having acceded to her boyfriend's request, and she said: "It was not easy. . . . But I felt it was the right thing to do. I had to give them (father and his girlfriend) space. . . . I moved out, because that is what I would have expected to happen to me. . . . It would not be nice for me to be happy while she is miserable because of the death of her child. . . . I am doing this out of ubuntu" (Baby P's mother, follow-up interview, February 16, 2010). Here we have the extraordinary situation of a very ill woman with her very ill baby, both probably having contracted the infection via the father. Though they have grown stronger, they remain extremely vulnerable; they move out to make space for father's girlfriend, so that she and the father may mourn the loss of their baby.

While our mother did not have much of a choice in this, she could have acquiesced and done what was expected of her while feeling angry about it. There was, however, no grudge in this young woman—she said she did this out of ubuntu. She was able to connect with the other on a personal or rather transpersonal level—from mother to mother. She imagined what it would have been like for her to be in a similar situation, and that empathy enabled her to accept the wish of the boy-friend without any negative feelings. She gave to the other woman not out of weakness but out of self-respect. She is not waiting for gratitude or thanks, but she is at peace with the knowledge that she acted according to a collective ethical principle. This is a small example, almost so small as to have gone unnoticed were it not for careful inquiry as to this young woman's equanimity in the face of a difficult life.

The second illustration comes from within the same community and could likewise have been overlooked within the bustle of a busy and noisy clinic setting. We had been seeing a young mother with her now nine-month-old baby for about half a year. The infant's weight had improved and I had asked her how we should proceed—wanting to give her the chance to say whether she wanted to terminate her regular contact with us or not. Her temporary employment had just come to an end, but she seemed determined to keep trying to find another position. This was her reply to my question:

"Because she [her daughter] is getting right, I should give another person a chance [to come to this clinic] . . . there are people who have nothing, we should not be greedy . . . we should give another person a chance" (O. P.'s mother, case notes, September 11, 2009). This is a very ordinary young mother struggling to make ends meet, possibly frustrated because she cannot find employment; yet despite this she is generous, she thinks of the other, a nameless, collective "other," for whom she stands back and shows caring.

These grassroots-level, day-to-day examples leave one humbled and amazed and convey the subtle quality of a set of values deeply embedded in the psyche of many people. Another moving account of ubuntu was given by Pumla Gobodo-Madikizela in her address about trauma and forgiveness, speaking at the seventeenth International Association for Analytical Psychology Conference in Cape Town in 2007 (Gobodo-Madikizela 2008).

Mbelo, a black policeman who was involved in the shooting of seven young men, known as the "Gugulethu Seven Killings," appeared in front of the Truth and Reconciliation Commission in 1996. He was facing the mothers of the young men. They were angry, accusing him of being a wolf dressed in sheep's clothing, of betraying his own blood, of selling his brothers' lives to white men. Mbelo begged the mothers for their forgiveness and said: "I would like to ask you to forgive me, my parents . . . I ask your forgiveness my parents" (in Gobodo-Madikizela 2008, 181). Gobodo-Madikizela observes that it might seem presumptuous for a man responsible for killing the sons of these women dares to refer to them as "my parents." She states that his choice of language "demonstrates the multidimensionality of social relationships with the African cultural context." In this sociocultural context the element of humanity is preserved in the way that persons are addressed—it is "inspired by the abiding humanity of ubuntu" (181).

The response of one of the mothers is equally stunning: "My son, you are the same age as my son, Christopher. I want to tell you today, that I as Christopher's mother, I forgive you my son" (in Gobodo-Madikizela 2008, 181). Her final words to Mbelo were "go well my child." These words "suggest an affirmation of the humanity that now binds Mbelo to her, and to some extent, the other mothers' own humanity" (181–82).

This ability to forgive comes deeply out of ubuntu—even though during the Truth and Reconciliation Commission this astounding capacity that became so visible may have been couched in terms of Christian forgiveness, it went beyond that. It is more than forgiveness on a personal, religious, super-ego level. It has to do with a much larger sense of forgiveness.

Forgiveness is part of ubuntu. A person who does not have the willingness to forgive would be lacking in ubuntu and would therefore have lost his or her humanity. Similarly, people who have acted against others, who have transgressed, cannot simply be discarded or given up on—they should be helped to mend their ways (Mnyaka 2003, 153). Not to forgive would be to ban that person from the human family, and this is something that is intolerable. This is much of what the TRC showed white South Africans and what it showed the world.

Describing the end of the Truth and Reconciliation Commission process, Krog writes:

> I am filled with an indescribable tenderness towards this Commission. . . . It has been so brave, so naively brave in the winds of deceit, rancour and hate. Against a flood crashing with the weight of a brutalizing past on the new usurping politics, the Commission has kept alive the idea of a common humanity. Painstakingly it has chiselled a way beyond racism and made a space for all of our voices. For its failures, it carries a flame of hope that makes me proud to be from here, of here. (Krog 1998, 278)

And it is of course the personal examples of the struggle heroes of the time that enabled much of this to unfold. Mandela's deep sense of ubuntu and South Africans' readiness to meet him and embrace these ideals has enabled South Africa to emerge out of its devastating times. In his speech at the final sitting of the first democratically elected Parliament in Cape Town on March 26, 1999, Mandela said:

> I have noted with deep gratitude, the generous praise that has often been given to me as an individual. But let me state this:
> To the extent that I have been able to achieve anything, I know that this is because I am the product of the people of South Africa.
> I am the product of the rural masses who inspired in me the pride in our past and the spirit of resistance.
> I am the product of the workers of South Africa, who, in the mines, factories, fields and offices of our country, have pursued the principle that the interests of each are founded in the common interest of all.
> I am the product of South Africa's intelligentsia, of every colour, who have laboured to give our society knowledge of itself and to fashion our people's aspirations into a realisable dream. . . .
> To the extent that I have been able to take our country forward to this new era it is because I am the product of the people of the world who have cherished the vision of a better life for all people everywhere. . . .
> I am the product of Africa and her long-cherished dream of a rebirth that can now be realised so that all of her children may play in the sun (in Asmal et al. 2003, 174).

Here is a truly beautiful illustration of this extraordinary human being at the height of his personal power placing himself firmly within collective humanity—the world, Africa, and all the layers of South Africa's peoples. It is a lived sense of ubuntu, one that Mandela has consistently conveyed. He has never taken praise personally; he has always situated himself within the context of his people. This is a humility and a humanity that is real, and that is evident—it permeates him as it does many others. This is beyond complex theory, this is something else—what it is, and where it fits into psychological theory, remains a question. Perhaps it is best located within the traditional African religious or spiritual attitude, as indeed Mandela and others have claimed.

Conclusion

Ubuntu in its African form no longer exists in Europe, but in Africa it has survived—it has not been made redundant. It finds expression in small and large ways. It is what makes southern Africa a place that tugs at the heart, despite all its problems. This ubuntu, this interconnectedness as human beings cannot be reduced; it defies usual theoretical categorization—it is something that simply *is*. It is a given, as Louw has stated—but it is also an ethical ideal, and therefore a task, something for which people can strive.

The need to participate with others, to work together, could be regarded as compensation for the increasingly common modern attitude of individualism with its abstract, reified thinking and its premium on self-fulfillment. Antjie Krog (Krog 2009b) goes so far as to say that this indigenous worldview of ubuntu could be regarded as a new moral entry point for the world. The sense that "community" goes beyond one's own could provide all of humanity with a radically new way of resolving complex matters. With development advancing globally and with an increasing premium being placed on individual well-being, there may well be the danger of this humanity getting lost, making the naming, the respecting, and the honoring of ubuntu all the more necessary.

Africa may not have sophisticated technology and successful financial markets, it may be afflicted by much hardship and suffering, but it does have an abundance of indigenous wealth—in its soil and in its humanity. Is it possible that Africa, the dark continent, could restore a balance to the world—that it could complement individualistic strivings with a spiritual and social attitude?

Nelson Mandela's words ring true, as he has done more than just speak them well; he has also truly lived them:

As with other aspects of its heritage, African traditional religion is increasingly recognised for its contribution to the world. No longer seen as despised superstition which had to be superseded by superior forms of belief, today its enrichment of humanity's spiritual heritage is acknowledged. The spirit of *Ubuntu*—that profound African sense that we are humans only through the humanity of other human beings—is not a parochial phenomenon, but has added globally to our common search for a better world" (in Asmal et al. 2003, 324).

Afterword

I have taken you with me on a journey to a place that is far away from here—far from the adult world, and from the scientific corridors of Europe and the United States. I have discussed babies, rituals and ceremonies, and an African worldview. What meaning can these things have for those of us immersed in western society and thought? Before suggesting how the three cohere, let me summarize the ground covered.

My point of entry was the baby: I have shown how the infant helped me to find a way to connect with persons and groups of people I would otherwise not have known as intimately as I do now.

Babies, however, could only help me provided I was able to enter their world, see it through their eyes. Once we can do this and once we realize the infants' abilities to perceive and take in their environment, we cannot but become activists on their behalf. The discovery of the complexity of the infant's brain, and the experience-dependent nature of its growth and development, serve as a wake-up call to mental health professionals, policy makers, and indeed politicians. We cannot make the world a better place if we do not take cognizance of the fact that those who are the future are deeply and severely affected by what they see, feel, and hear in their early life. If our young bear the brunt of warfare and deprivation, then we cannot be surprised that cycles of violence and recrimination perpetuate themselves for generations.

As much as infants are affected by what goes on around them, so they are also embedded in the culture from which they come. This deeper layer, this cultural conscious and unconscious, was opened to me through my work with very young patients. The case of little Athi was my personal wake-up call—it made me realize that superficial knowledge of another's culture is not enough; certainly not enough when one has to fulfill the function of a psychotherapist and patient manager.

Through him, and also through the role Vera Bührmann played in my life, I was motivated to understand more about the *Weltanschauung* of the amaXhosa group of people in my country. The concept of ancestor reverence and the rituals to which it gives rise have deep meaning even today, and even in an urbanized, modern setting. Similarly, the adolescent rite of passage for boys persists as a definite and incisive act of separation away from the mother into the world of men. Old-fashioned as this may sound on one level, on another level it provides the male child with an opportunity to individuate in a way that is not easily approximated in the West. Last, the concept of ubuntu is moving and staggering in its simplicity and complexity. If the world could have more ubuntu it might become a better place.

The *leitmotiv* throughout these lectures has been "from small to big and from big to small." It forms an arc—it forms a bridge that connects us to ourselves and to the other. Unless we can comprehend

Nelson Mandela with Kofi Anan of the United Nations, July 2007; Mandela's deep sense of ubuntu helped lead all South Africans out of devastating times.

the small in the big and the big in the small we will not see the whole picture, and we will not grasp either ourselves or the other person.

We can only build a bridge to the other side—whoever and whatever that other side might be—if we start off on the same level, if we start small. If we come from a superior, inflated position we will not meet as equals in the middle.

We need to have the correct attitude; we need to know who we are, where we come from, and what it is in us that motivates and drives us—in other words, we have to own the personal equation, which includes what we project onto others that has stopped us from seeing them. This withdrawal of projections is a huge task. Jung has written extensively about the assimilation of the shadow. I have not focused much on what our shadow is in the western world, what it is that we have to own. I have concentrated rather on what wealth, what riches there are in the other, from the baby to the adult—if only we can open ourselves to a different way of thinking, a different way of looking. Once we can appreciate what the other (small or big) has to offer, and what we can learn, then the withdrawal of projections may occur almost spontaneously—this has been my personal experience and that of many other South Africans.

The world is in a fraught place. There are painful, conflict-laden areas in many countries where bloodshed and the suffering of young and old are immeasurably painful. With instant communication, with immediate visual display of what is occurring in the most remote areas of our globe, surely we all become part of the whole—members of one big human family. If that is so, then "a person is a person because of persons" is not merely an old African concept that intrigues writers and philosophers but an injunction to us all. It is this that binds together what I have tried to convey in this Fay Lecture Series and in this book.

References

Alanis, M. C., and R. S. Lucidi. 2004. Neonatal Circumcision: A Review of the
World's Oldest and Most Controversial Operation. *Obstetrical and Gyneco-
logical Survey* 59 (5): 379 95.

Almond, P. 2009. Postnatal Depression: A Global Public Health Perspective.
Perspect. Public Health 129 (5): 221–27.

ANC Commission for Religious Affairs. 2006. From Liberation to Transformation: Spiritual Revolution in a Secular Society. *Umrabulo* 27. http://www.anc.
org.za/show.php?include=docs/umrabulo/2006/umrabul027.html.

Asmal, K., D. Chidester, and W. James. 2003. *Nelson Mandela: From Freedom to
the Future—Tributes and Speeches.* Johannesburg: Jonathan Ball Publishers.

Auerbach, J. S., and S. J. Blatt. Self-Reflexivity, Intersubjectivity, and Therapeutic
Change. *Psychoanalytic Psychology* 18: 427–50.

Baradon, T. 2005. "What Is Genuine Maternal Love"? Clinical Considerations
and Technique in Psychoanalytic Parent-Infant Psychotherapy. *Psychoanalytic Study of the Child* 60: 47–73.

Barbarin, O., and L. M. Richter. 2001. *Mandela's Children: Growing up in Post-
Apartheid South Africa.* London: Routledge.

Berg, A. 2002a. Talking with Infants: A Bridge to Cross-Cultural Intervention.
Southern African Journal of Child and Adolescent Mental Health 14 (1): 5–14.

———. 2002b.Ubuntu: From the Consulting Room to the Vegetable Garden. In
Between Sessions and Beyond the Couch, ed. J. Raphael Leff. Colchester, U.K.:
CPS Psychoanalytic Publications. Pp. 102–107.

———. 2003a. Beyond the Dyad: Parent-Infant Psychotherapy in a Multicultural Society—Reflections from a South African Perspective. *Infant Mental
Health Journal* 24 (3): 265–77.

———. 2003b. Ancestor Reverence and Mental Health in South Africa. *Transcultural Psychiatry* 40 (2): 194–297.

———. 2004. *Ubuntu*—A Contribution to the "Civilization of the Universal."
In *The Cultural Complex: Contemporary Jungian Perspectives on Psyche and Society,* eds. T. Singer and S. L. Kimbles. Hove: Brunner-Routledge. Pp. 239–50.

———. 2007. Can We Prevent Colonization of the Mind? Traditional Culture in South Africa. In *Who Owns Jung?* ed. Ann Casement. London: Karnac. Pp. 93–110.

Berinyuu, A. A. 2002. An African Therapy in Dialogue with Freudian Psychoanalysis. *Journal of Pastoral Care and Counseling* 56 (1): 11–20.

Bion, W. R. 1962. *Learning from Experience.* London: Maresfield Library.

Broodryk, J. 2002. *Ubuntu—Life Lessons from Africa.* Pretoria: Ubuntu School of Philosophy.

Bührmann, M. V. 1978. Tentative Views on Dream Therapy by Xhosa Diviners. *Journal of Analytical Psychology* 23 (2): 105–21.

———. 1981. The Xhosa Healers of Southern Africa, pt. 1, Intlombe and Xhentsa: A Xhosa Healing Ritual. *Journal of Analytical Psychology* 26: 187–201.

———. 1984. *Living in Two Worlds.* Cape Town: Human and Rousseau.

Campbell-Hall, V., I. Petersen, A. Bhana, S. Mjadu, V. Hosegood, and A. J. Flisher. 2010. Collaboration between Traditional Practitioners and Primary Health Care Staff in South Africa: Developing a Workable Partnership for Community Mental Health Services. *Transcultural Psychiatry* 47 (4): 610–28.

Clachterty and Associates. 2003. *Soul Buddyz 3 Audience Research: Girls' and Boys Perception of Masculinity.* Auckland Park: Education and Social Development.

Constitution of the Republic of South Africa. Act 200 of 1993. Chap 15. *http://www.info.gov.za/documents/constitution/93cons.htm#.*

Crowley, I. P., and K. M. Kesner. 1990. Ritual Circumcision (Umkhwetha) amongst the Xhosa of the Ciskei. *British Journal of Urology* 66: 318–21.

David, D. H., and K. Lyons-Ruth. 2005. Differential Attachment Responses of Male and Female Infants to Frightening Maternal Behaviour: Tend or Befriend versus Fight or Flight? *Infant Mental Health Journal* 26 (1): 1–18.

d'Errico, F., M. Vanhaeren, N. Barton, A. Bouzouggar, H. Mienis, D. Richter, et al. 2000. Out of Africa—Modern Human Origins Special Feature: Additional Evidence on the Use of Personal Ornaments in the Middle Paleolithic of North Africa. *Proc. Natl. Acad. Sci. USA* 106 (38): 16051–56.

deMause, L. 1974. The Evolution of Childhood. In *The History of Childhood: The Evolution of Parent-Child Relationships as a Factor in History,* ed. L. deMause. London: Souvenir Press. Pp. 1–74.

Dreifuss, G. 1965. A Psychological Study of Circumcision in Judaism. *Journal of Analytical Psychology* 10 (1): 23–32.

Edinger, E. F. 1960. The Ego-Self Paradox. *Journal of Analytical Psychology* 5: 3–18.

Emde, R. N. 2006. Culture, Diagnostic Assessment, and Identity: Defining Concepts. *Infant Mental Health Journal* 27 (6): 606–11.

Evarts, A. B. 1919. Color Symbolism. *Psychoanalytic Review* 6: 124–57.

Fonagy, P. 1998. Prevention, the Appropriate Target of Infant Psychotherapy. *Infant Mental Health Journal* 19 (2): 124–50.

Freud, S. 1974. *Introductory Lectures on Psychoanalysis.* Pelican Freud Library ed. Harmondsworth, U.K.: Penguin Books.

Funani, L. S. 1990. *Circumcision among the Ama-Xhosa: A Medical Investigation.* Braamfontein: Skotaville Publishers.

Giegerich, W. 2004. The End of Meaning and the Birth of Man: An Essay about the State Reached in the History of Consciousness and Analysis of C. G. Jung's Psychology Project. *Journal of Jungian Theory and Practice* 6 (1): 1–66.

Grantham-McGregor, S., Y. B. Cheung, S. Cuteo, P. Glewwe, L. Richter B. Strupp, et al. 2007. Developmental Potential in the First 5 years for Children in Developing Countries. *Lancet* 369: 60–70.

Gobodo-Madikizela, P. 2008. Trauma, Forgiveness and the Witnessing Dance: Making Public Spaces Intimate. *Journal of Analytical Psychology* 53 (2): 169–88.

Hammond-Tooke, W. D. 1937. World-View II: A System of Action. In *The Bantu-Speaking Peoples of Southern Africa,* ed. W. D. Hammond-Tooke. London: Routledge and Kegan Paul. Pp. 344–63.

Harris, M., and E. Bick. 1976. The Contribution of Observation of Mother-Infant Interaction and Development to the Equipment of a Psychoanalyst or Psychoanalytic Psychotherapist. *Collected Papers of Martha Harris and Esther Bick.* Perthshire, Scotland: Clunie Press. Pp. 225–39.

Hobson, R. F. 1961. Critical Notices: *The Archetypes and the Collective Unconscious,* by C. G. Jung, translated by R. F. C. Hull, in *Collected Works,* vol. 9, pt. 1. (London: Routledge and Kegan Paul, 1959), i-xi, 1–462). *Journal of Analytical Psychology* 6: 161–69.

Jacoby, M. 1999. *Jungian Psychotherapy and Contemporary Infant Research.* London: Routledge.

Johnson, M. H. 2005. Subcortical Face Processing. *Nat. Rev. Neurosci.* 6 (10): 766–74.

Jung, C. G. 1917. *Collected Works of C. G. Jung,* vol. 7: *Two Essays on Analytical Psychology.* 2nd ed., 1966, Princeton: Princeton University Press.

———. 1959. The Psychology of the Child Archetype. In *Collected Works of C. G. Jung,* vol. 9, pt. 1: *The Archetypes and the Collective Unconscious.* Princeton: Princeton University Press. Pp. 151–81.

———. 1963. *Memories, Dreams and Reflections.* London: Collins.

———. 1969a. *Psychology and Religion: West and East.* 2nd ed. London: Routledge and Kegan Paul.

———. 1969b. *The Structure and Dynamics of the Psyche.* 2nd ed. London: Routledge and Kegan Paul.

———. 1976. *Symbols of Transformation.* 2nd ed. Princeton: Princeton University Press.

———. 1977. *The Archetypes and the Collective Unconscious.* Princeton: Princeton University Press.

Kepe, T. 2010. "Secrets" That Kill: Crisis, Custodianship and Responsibility in Ritual Male Circumcision in the Eastern Cape Province, South Africa. *Social Science and Medicine* 70: 729–35.

Kisilevsky, B. S., S. M. Hains, C. A. Brown, C. T. Lee, B. Cowperthwaite, S. S. Stutzman, et al. 2009. Fetal Sensitivity to Properties of Maternal Speech and Language. *Infant Behav. Development* 32 (1): 59–71.

Knox, J. 2003. *Archetype, Attachment, Analysis: Jungian Psychology and the Emergent Mind.* Hove: Brunner-Routledge.

Krog, A. 1998. *Country of My Skull.* Cape Town: Random House.

———. 2009a. *Begging to Be Black.* Cape Town: Random House–Struik.

———. 2009b. Comments at Beyond Reconciliation Conference, December 2–9, University of Cape Town.

Kurjak, A., M. Stanojevic, W. Andonotopo, A. Salihagic-Kadic, and J. M. Carrera, and G. Azumendi. 2004. Behavioral Pattern Continuity from Prenatal to Postnatal Life: A Study by Four-Dimensional (4D) Ultrasonography. *Journal of Perinatal Medicine* 32 (4): 346–53.

Lagercrantz, H., and J. P. Changeux. 2009. The Emergence of Human Consciousness: From Fetal to Neonatal Life. *Pediatr. Res.* 65 (3): 255–60.

Lamberg, B. R. 1981. Eye Opening of the Newborn at and up to 20 Minutes after Birth. *Journal of Advanced Nursing* 16 (6): 455–59.

Laye, C. 1954. *The African Child*. Glasgow: Fontana-Collins.

Lecanuet, J.P., and B. Schaal. 1996. Fetal Sensory Competencies. *Eur. J. Obstet. Gynecol. Reprod. Biol.* 6 (1–2): 1–23.

Levi-Strauss C. 1963. *Structural Anthropology*. London: Allen Lane–Penguin Press.

Louw, D. J. 2002. *Ubuntu and the Challenges of Multiculturalism in Post-Apartheid South Africa.* 2002. Utrecht: University of Utrecht, Expertisecentrum Zuidelijk Afrika.

Maiello, S. 1995. The Sound-Object: A Hypothesis about Prenatal Auditory Experience and Memory. *Journal of Child Psychotherapy* 21 (1): 23–41.

———. 1997. Interplay: Sound-Aspects in Mother-Infant Observation. In *Developments in Infant Observation: The Tavistock Model,* ed. S. Reid. London: Routledge. Pp. 157–73.

———. 2000. The Cultural Dimension in Early Mother-Infant Interaction and Psychic Development: An Infant Observation in South Africa. *International Journal of Infant Observation and Its Applications* 3 (29): 80–92.

Marlier, L., B. Schaal, and R. Soussignan. 1998. Neonatal Responsiveness to the Odor of Amniotic and Lacteal Fluids: A Test of Perinatal Chemosensory Continuity. *Child Development* 69 (3): 611–23.

McBrearty, S., and A. Brooks. 2000. The Revolution That Wasn't: A New Interpretation of the Origin of Modern Human Behavior. *J. Hum. Evol.* 39 (5): 453–563.

Meintjies, G. 1998. *Manhood at a Price: Socio-Medical Perspectives on Xhosa Traditional Circumcision.* Institute of Social and Economic Research, ISER Working Papers.

Meintjies, H., and S. Giese. 2006. Spinning the Epidemic: The Making of Mythologies of Orphanhood in the Context of AIDS. *Childhood* 13 (3): 407–30.

Meissner, O., and D. L. Buso. 2007. Traditional Male Circumcision in the Eastern Cape: Scourge or Blessing? *S. Afr. Med. J.* 97: 371–73.

Meltzoff, A. N., and R. W. Borton. 1979. Intermodal Matching by Human Neonates. *Nature* 282 (5737): 403–404.

Mgqolozana, T. 2009. *A Man Who Is Not a Man.* Scottsville: University of KwaZulu-Natal Press.

Mkhize, N. 2006. African Traditions and the Social, Economic and Moral Dimensions of Fatherhood. In *Baba: Men and Fatherhood in South Africa,* ed. L. Richter and R. Morrell. Cape Town: HSRC Press. Pp. 183–98.

Mndende, N. 2006. *An Introduction to African Religion.* Cape Town: Printing Press.

Mnyaka, M. M. N. 2003. Xenophobia as a Response to Foreigners in Post-Apartheid South Africa and Post-Exilic Israel: A Comparative Critique in the Light of the Gospel and Ubuntu Ethical Principles. Dissertation, University of South Africa, Pretoria.

Morgan, A. 2007. What I Am Trying to Do When I See the Infant with His or Her Parents. In *The Baby as Subject,* ed. F. Thomson Salo and C. Paul. 2nd ed. Melbourne: Stonnington Press. Pp. 12–17.

Morrell, R. 1998. Of Boys and Men: Masculinity and Gender in Southern African Studies. *Journal of Southern African Studies* 24 (4): 605–30.

Neumann, E. 1954. *The Origins and History of Consciousness.* Princeton: Princeton University Press.

———. 1973. *The Child.* Boston: Shambhala.

Ngxamngxa, A. N. N. 1971. The Function of Circumcision among the Xhosa-speaking Tribes in Historical Perspective. In *Man: Anthropological Essays Presented to O. F. Raum,* ed. E. J. de Jager. Cape Town: C. Struik. Pp. 183–204.

Nietzsche, F. 1964. *Also sprach Zarathustra.* Stuttgart: Kröner Verlag.

Norman, J. 2001. The Psychoanalyst and the Baby: A New Look at Work with Infants. *International Journal of Psychoanalysis* 82: 83–100.

Nqweni, Z. C. 1999. Group Analytic Psychotherapy, with Specific Reference to the Structure of Western and Traditional Psychotherapy Groups. In *Cross-Cultural Dialogue on Psychotherapy in Africa,* ed. S. N. Madu, P. K. Baguma, and A. Pritz. Sovenga, South Africa: University of the North Press. Pp. 184–92.

Perry, B. D., R. A. Pollard, T. L. Blakley, W. L. Baker, and D. Vigilante D. 1995. Childhood Trauma, the Neurobiology of Adaptation, and "Use-Dependent" Development of the Brain: How "States" Become "Traits." *Infant Mental Health Journal* 16 (4): 271–91.

Piontelli, A. 1992. *From Fetus to Child: An Observational Psychoanalytic Study.* London: Routledge.

Preston-Whyte, E. 1937. Kinship and Marriage. In *The Bantu-Speaking Peoples of Southern Africa,* ed. W. D. Hammond-Tooke. London: Routledge and Kegan Paul. Pp. 177–210.

Preston-Whyte, E., and M. Zondi. 1996. African Teenage Pregnancy: Whose Problem? In Questionable Issue: Illegitimacy in South Africa, ed. S. Burman and E. Preston-Whyte. Cape Town: Oxford University Press. Pp. 226–46.

Ramphele, M. 2008. *Laying Ghosts to Rest—Dilemmas of the Transformation in South Africa*. Paarl: Tafelberg.

Roland, A. 1996. How Universal Is the Psychoanalytic Self? In Reaching across Boundaries of Culture and Class: Widening the Scope of Psychotherapy, ed. P, R. M. Foster, M. Mokowitz, and R. A. Javier. Northvale, N.J.: Jason Aronson. Pp. 71–90.

Rossi, E. 1977. The Cerebral Hemispheres in Analytical Psychology. *Journal of Analytical Psychology* 22 (32): 51.

Salo, F. T. 2007. Recognizing the Infant as Subject in Infant-Parent Psychotherapy. *International Journal of Psychoanalysis* 88 (4): 961–79.

Schore, A. N. 2001. Effects of a Secure Attachment Relationship on Right Brain Development, Affect Regulation, and Infant Mental Health. *Infant Mental Health Journal* 22 (1–2): 7–66.

———. 2002. Dysregulation of the Right Brain: A Fundamental Mechanism of Traumatic Attachment and the Psychopathogenesis of Posttraumatic Stress Disorder [review]. *Australian and New Zealand Journal of Psychiatry* 36 (1): 9–30.

Schwarzer, G., and H. Leder. 2003. *The Development of Face Processing*. Göttingen: Hogrefe and Huber.

Shapiro, V., S. Fraiberg, and E. Adelson. 1976. Infant-Parent Psychotherapy on Behalf of a Child in a Critical Nutritional State. *Psychoanalytic Study of the Child* 31: 461–91.

Shaw, M. 1937. Material Culture. In *The Bantu-Speaking Peoples of Southern Africa*, ed. W. D. Hammond-Tooke. London: Routledge and Kegan Paul. Pp. 85–134.

Singer, T., and S. L. Kimbles. 2004. *The Cultural Complex: Contemporary Jungian Perspectives on Psyche and Society*. Hove: Brunner-Routledge.

Spitz, R. 1946. Anaclitic Depression: An Inquiry into the Genesis of Psychiatric Conditions in Early Childhood, pt. 2. *Psychoanalytic Study of the Child* 2: 313–42.

Stern, D. N. 1985. *The Interpersonal World of the Infant: A View from Psychoanalysis and Developmental Psychology*. New York: Basic Books.

———. 2002. *The First Relationship*. Cambridge, Mass.: Harvard University Press.

Swartz, L. 1996. Culture and Mental Health in the Rainbow Nation: Transcultural Psychiatry in a Changing South Africa. *Transcultural Psychiatric Research Review* 33: 119–36.

————. 1998. *Culture and Mental Health: A Southern African View.* Cape Town: Oxford University Press.

Tattersall, I. 2009. Out of Africa—Modern Human Origins Special Feature: Human Origins, Out of Africa. *Proc. Natl. Acad. Sci. USA* 106 (38): 16018–21.

Taylor, J. V. 1963. *The Primal Vision: Christian Presence amid African Religion.* London: SCM Press.

Turner, V. 1987. The Liminal Period in Rites of Passage. In *Betwixt and Between: Patterns of Masculine and Feminine Initiation,* ed. L. Mahdi, S. Foster, and M. Little. La Salle, Ill.: Open Court. Pp. 3–22.

Tutu, D. 2005. *God Has a Dream: A Vision of Hope for Our Time.* London: Rider.

van der Vliet, V. 1974. Growing up in Traditional Society. In *The Bantu-speaking Peoples of Southern Africa,* ed. W. D. Hammond-Tooke. London: Routledge and Kegan Paul. Pp. 211–34.

van Gennep, A. 1960. *The Rites of Passage.* London: Routledge.

Vincent, L. 2008. "Boys Will Be Boys": Traditional Xhosa Male Circumcision, HIV and Sexual Socialisation in Contemporary South Africa. *Culture, Health and Sexuality* 10 (5): 431–46.

von Klitzing, K., H. Simoni, and D. Bürgin. 1999. Child Development and Early Triadic Relationships. Pt. 1. *International Journal of Psychoanalysis* 80: 71–89.

Wiener, J. 2009. *The Therapeutic Relationship: Transference, Countertransference, and the Making of Meaning.* College Station: Texas A&M University Press.

Winnicott, D. W. 1971. *Playing and Reality.* Harmondsworth, England: Penguin Books.

————. 1990. *The Maturational Process and the Facilitating Environment.* London: Karnac.

Wissow, L. S. 1998. Infanticide. *New England Journal of Medicine* 339 (17): 1239–41.

Index

archetypes
    archetypal inheritance, 25
    child archetypes, 33–35
    and "deliverance from the
        mother," 88–91
    and mother/child connection,
        25–26, *26*, 86
    and parental roles, 91–92
*Archetypes and the Collective Uncon-
    scious* (Jung), 25
assegai, 80
Athenkosi ("Athi"; child subject)
    and ancestor reverence, 53
    case overview, 38–42
    and cultural awareness, 117–18
    and cultural isolation, 44–45, *45*
    and cultural transgression,
        45–47
    genogram of, *38*
    lessons learned from, 49–51
    and manhood rituals, 78
    progress after case, 47–48,
        48–49
    and rites of passage, 69, 72, 74
    and western clinical perspec-
        tives, 42–44
attachment, 30, 42, 50
Attis, 89
auditory cortex, *21*
autism, 3–4, 40, 42
Ayanda, 73–74

Baby P, 109–10
baptism rituals, 76
bar mitzvahs, 82
Bick, E., 55
Bion, W. R., 61
bipolar complexes, 99
blood ties, 44
bonding issues, 43, *43*, 49–50
Borton, R. W., 24
braaivleis, 96

brain physiology and development
    and abilities of infants, 20–21,
        117
    and communicating with
        infants, 23, 26–30, *27*
    development rates, *21*
    and mother/child connection,
        86
breastfeeding, *24*, 29–30, 38
bridge-building
    and Bührmann, 3–6
    and infants, 20, 22, 34, 35–36,
        117
    Jung on, *13*, 20
    and "small-to-big" theme, 6, 20,
        118–19
    and subjectivity/objectivity, 2–3
Broca's area, *21*
Brooks, Alison, 106
Bührmann, Vera
    on African religion, 55
    and bridge-building, 3–7
    and cultural awareness, 118
    on dreams, 64
    and research practices, 54–56,
        78
    and ritual practices, 5–6, 61–62,
        63–64, 66
    and South African academic
        environment, 67
burial practices, 60
burn trauma, 38–39

Cape Flats, 12
Cape Town, 6, 9–10, 78
Catholicism, 75–76, 101
chants, 73
children and childhood. *See also*
    Athenkosi; infants
    and ancestor reverence, 72–74
    child archetypes, 33–35
    child psychiatry, 6, 10–11

and illegitimacy, 39–42, *43*, 44, 45–46
individuation of the child, 34, 69–72, 89, 118
and mother/child connection, 25–26, *26*, 86
rituals of, 44
and traumatic injuries, 38–42
and *ubuntu*, 98
children's homes, 48–49
Christianity, 53–54, 104–5, 112
Church Missionary Society, 104
circumcision practices, 68–69, 78, *79*, 79–82, 82–83, 89
clan affiliations, 73, 75
class issues, 10, 19
cogito ergo sum, 102, 107
cognitive functions, *21*, 117
collective human history, 33
collective psyche, 17, 95, 99
collective unconscious, 25–26
colonialism, 1, 67, 84, 91–92
communal relations, 16, 53–56, 62–63, 104–5
Conference on Infant Mental Health, 9–10
confirmations, 82
consciousness
collective unconscious, 25–26
and cultural values, 54
and fetal development, 24
self-consciousness, 26–27, 70, 101–3, 104–5
Constitution of South Africa, 99–100
containment concept, 61
core self, 24
cosmology, 54
counter-transference, 28, 31, 32
cows, 75–76
Creator, 60, 97
crime, 56–57
crisis of masculinity, 85

cultural values. *See also* ancestor reverence
and change, 91
and childhood development, 117
context of, 49–51, 53
and cultural bias, 38, 103, 104
and cultural complexes, 94–96, 98–101
and cultural isolation, 44–45
and the cultural unconscious, 54
and infant identity, 73
and isolation, 44–45, *45*, 47
multiculturalism, 67–69
and rites of passage, 57, 91–92
and scholarly research, 55
and separation anxiety, 17
and western clinical perspectives, 38, 42–44
Cybele, 89

dance, 58, 63–64, *79*, 103
death and rebirth themes, 89–91
"deliverance from the mother," 88–91
deMause, L., 31
democracy in South Africa, 9, 99–100
dependence, 22, 33
depression, 28, 30, 34
deprivation, 29–30
Descartes, René, 101–2, 104, 107
diversity of South Africa, 1, 49, 54
dreams, 63–64
Dutch East India Company, 78

Eastern Cape, 12, 72, 78
ego, 105
ego-self axis, 54–55, *55*, *97*
Egyptian culture, 78
elections, 100
emigration to South Africa, 7
empathy, 41, 110

and social connectedness,
64–66
hearing, *21,* 23, 26
Hedges, Nick, *13*
helplessness, 33
hero myths, 86–87, 88–91
HIV/AIDS, 85, 109–10
Hobson, R. F., 25
housing developments, 12
Human Sciences Research Council, 85
humility, 113–14

id, 105
illegitimacy of children, 39 *12, 13, 14,*
45–46
image schema, 25–26
imbeleko ritual, 6, 74–77, 79
imperialism, 84. *See also* colonialism
incest taboo, 72, 86–88
individualism
    and African religion, 54, 66
    and ancestor reverence, 17, *61,*
        73, 76–77, 97
    and cultural differences, 16
    and the hero myth, 87
    individuation of children, 34,
        69–72, 89, 118
    and social isolation, 44–45
    and *ubuntu,* 93–95, 114
    and the western psyche, 102–3,
        105
indlavini, 85
Infant Mental Health Conference, 9
Infant Mental Health Service, 39
infants
    abilities of, 20–26, *24,* 26–27
    and brain development, 20–21,
        26–30, 117
    and bridge-building, 3, 6, 20,
        35–36, 117
    communicating with, 23,
        26–30, *27*

failure to thrive, 29
    and individuation, 69–72
infanticide, 42
infant observation methods, 55
    and separation anxiety, 71–72
    and traditional parental roles,
        84
    and *ubuntu,* 94, 106–8, 109–11
ingcibi, 80, 89
inhlawulo, 45–46
initiations, 78. *See also* rituals and
    ceremonies
injuries to children, 38–42
inkedama, 108
intambo, 74–75, 76–77
interdependence, 93–94, 108, 114. *See*
    also ubuntu
International Association for Analyti-
    cal Psychology, 7, 111
intlombe ritual, 6, 56, 61–62, *63,*
    63–64, 65
iqhirha, 57–58
isiko, 61
isithethe, 61

Jacoby, M., 25
Johannesburg, 9
Judaism, 82, 90
Jung, Carl
    and abandonment trauma,
        34–35
    and archetypes, 25
    and "assimilation of the
        shadow," 119
    and the child archetype, 33–35
    and "deliverance from the
        mother," 89
    and mandala, 62
    and mother/child connection,
        86
    and the objective psyche, 105
    and Oedipal conflict, 70–71, *71*